DERBY·DERBY·DERBY·DERBY

ESTATE PUBLICATIONS
Bridewell House,
Tenterden, Kent.
TN30 6EP
Tel: 01580 764225

Loscoe
22   23
HEANOR

Duffield
26

7
Little
Eaton

Allestree
8   9   10   Breadsall   Oakwood
Markeaton   Chaddesden   11

6
DERBY
12   13   Spondon   Ockbrook
Mickleover 14   15   16   17
                              Borrowash

Normanton   Alvaston
18   19 20 Osmaston   21   27
            Sinfin   Draycott
Findern   Allenton
                27
                Chellaston

Lockington
CASTLE
DONINGTON
24   25

M1

ROAD MAP   page 4-5
ENLARGED CENTRE   page 6
STREET INDEX   page 28

E S T A T E   P U B L I C A T I O N S

DERBY

HEANOR · DUFFIELD · CASTLE DONINGTON
MICKLEOVER · CHELLASTON · BORROWASH

Every effort has been made to verify the accuracy of information in this book but the publishers cannot accept responsibility for expense or loss caused by any error or omission. Information that will be of assistance to the user of the maps will be welcomed.

The representation of a road, track or footpath on the maps in this atlas is no evidence of the existence of a right of way.

One-way Street	←
Car Park	℗
Place of Worship	✚
Post Office	●
Public Convenience	☉
Pedestrianized	▨

Scale of street plans 3½ inches to 1 mile
Unless otherwise stated

Street plans prepared and published by ESTATE PUBLICATIONS, Bridewell House, TENTERDEN, KENT, and based upon the ORDNANCE SURVEY maps with the sanction of the Controller of H. M. Stationery Office.

The Publishers acknowledge the co-operation of Amber Valley D.C., South Derbyshire D.C., Erewash D.C. and Derby D.C. in the preparation of these maps.

Ⓓ Estate Publications 179 G   ISBN 0 86084 747 0

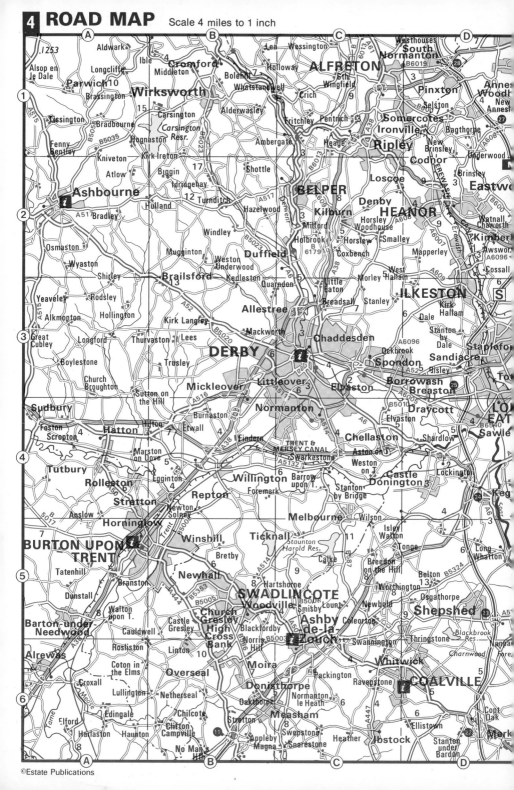

4 ROAD MAP

Scale 4 miles to 1 inch

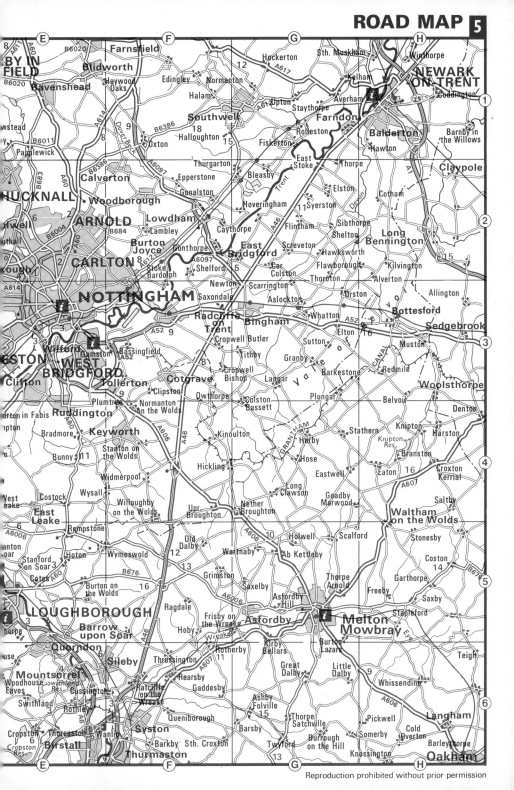

Scale

0   ¼

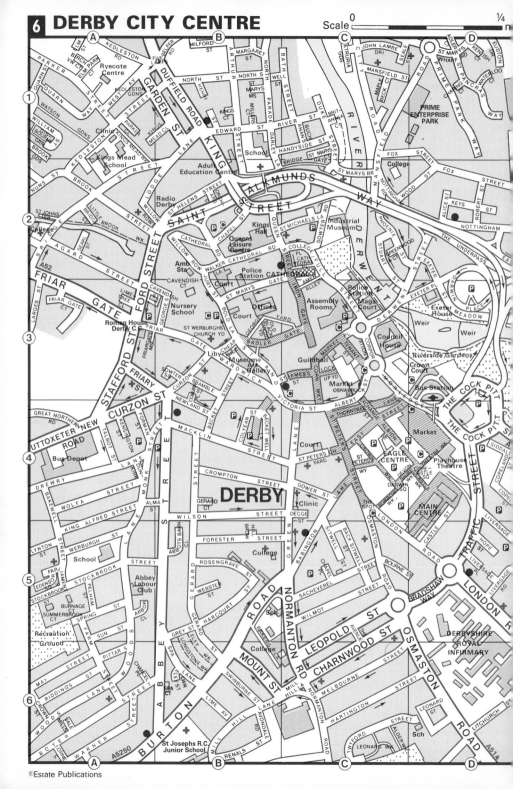

©Estate Publications

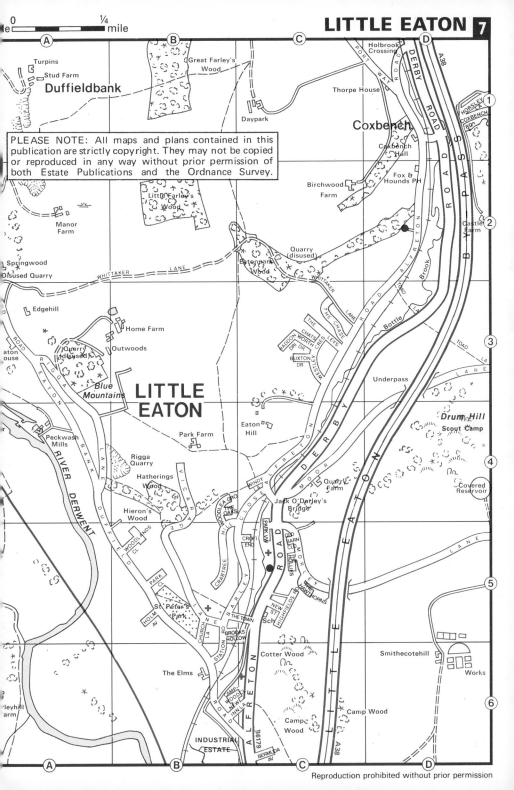

LITTLE EATON 7

PLEASE NOTE: All maps and plans contained in this publication are strictly copyright. They may not be copied or reproduced in any way without prior permission of both Estate Publications and the Ordnance Survey.

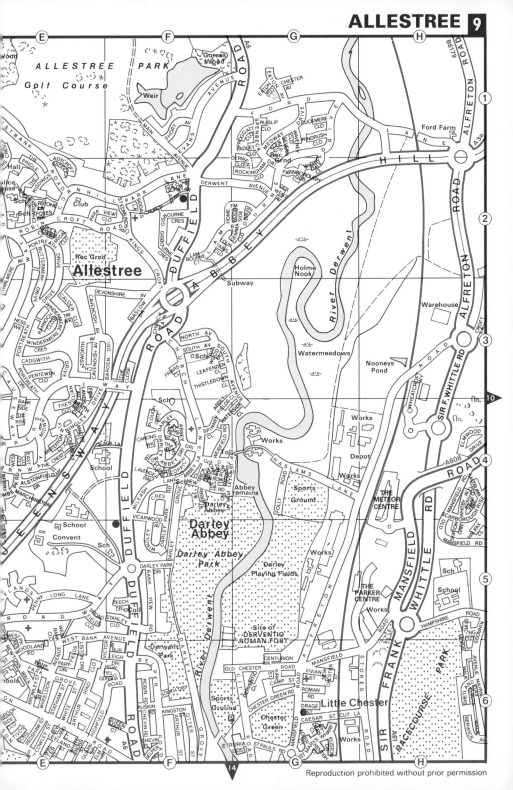

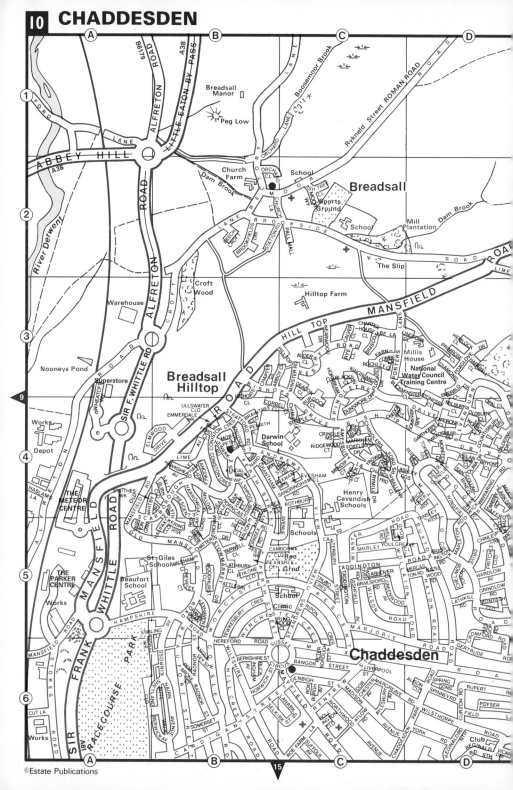

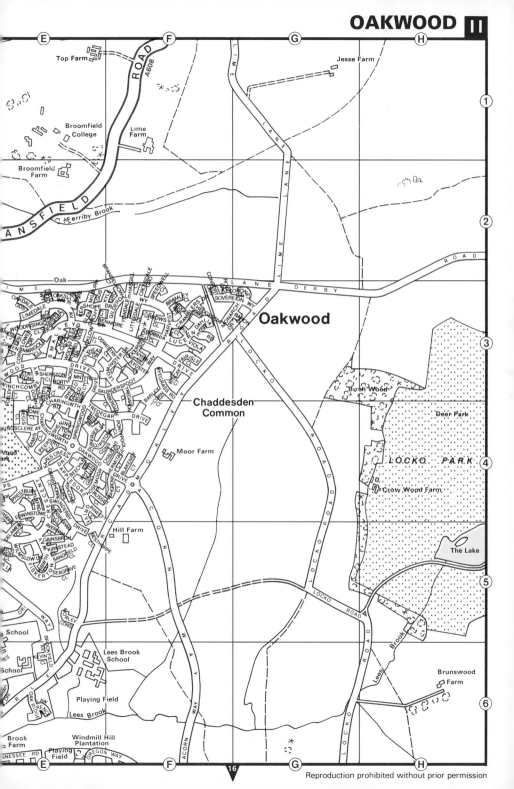

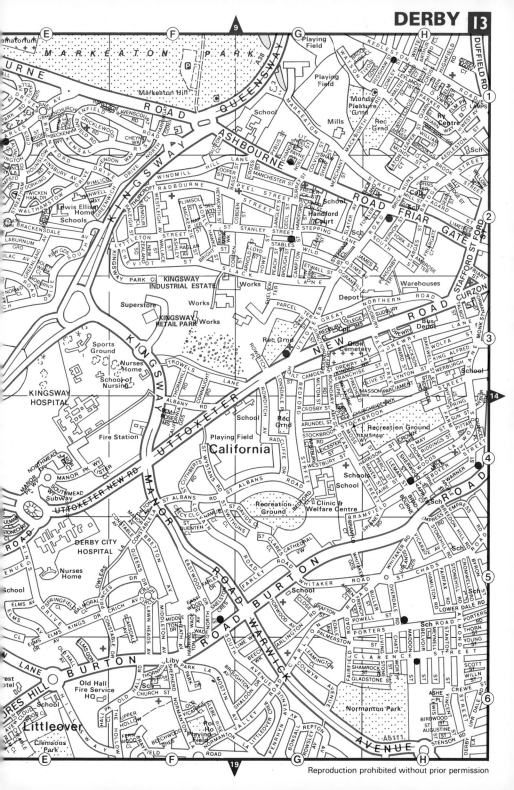

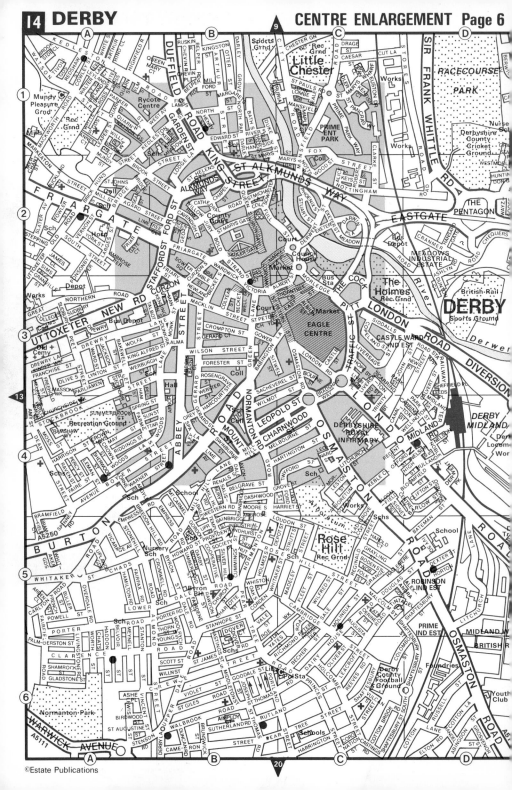

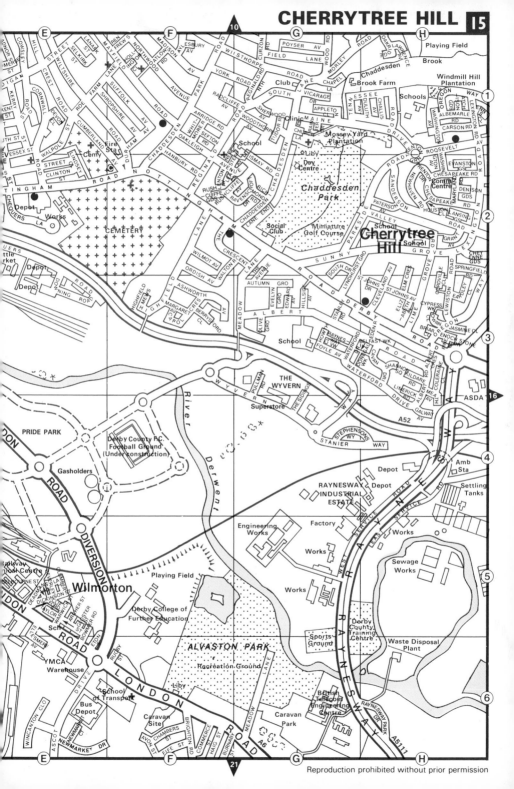

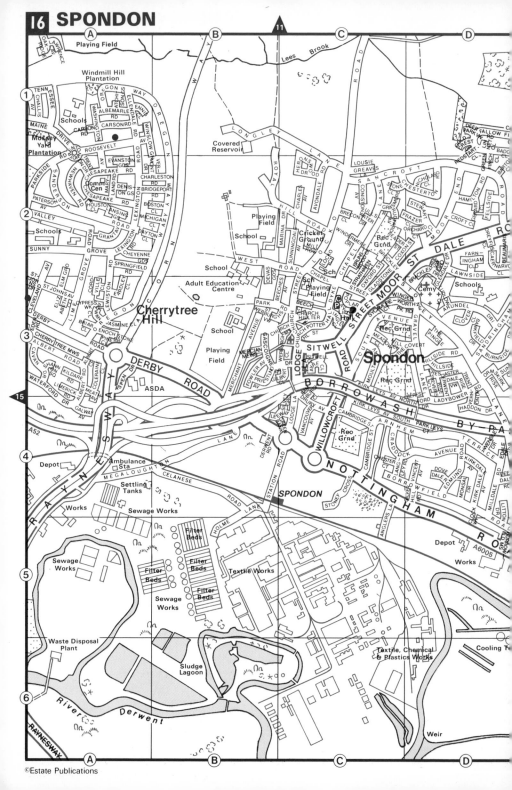

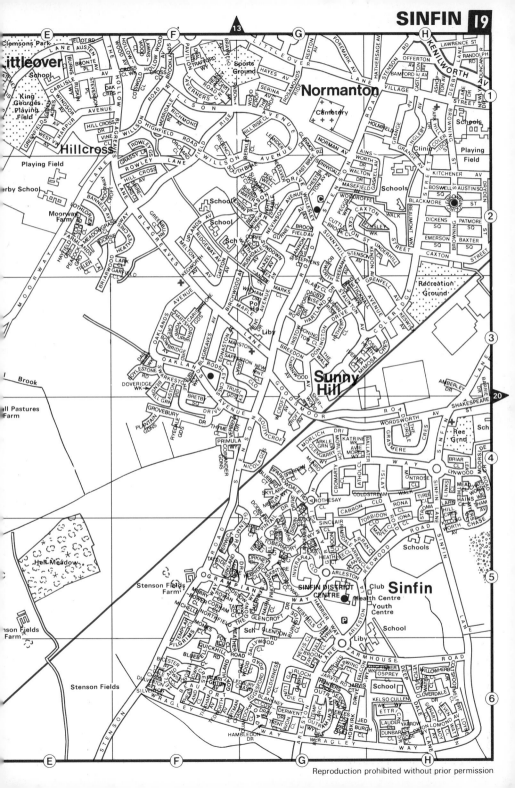

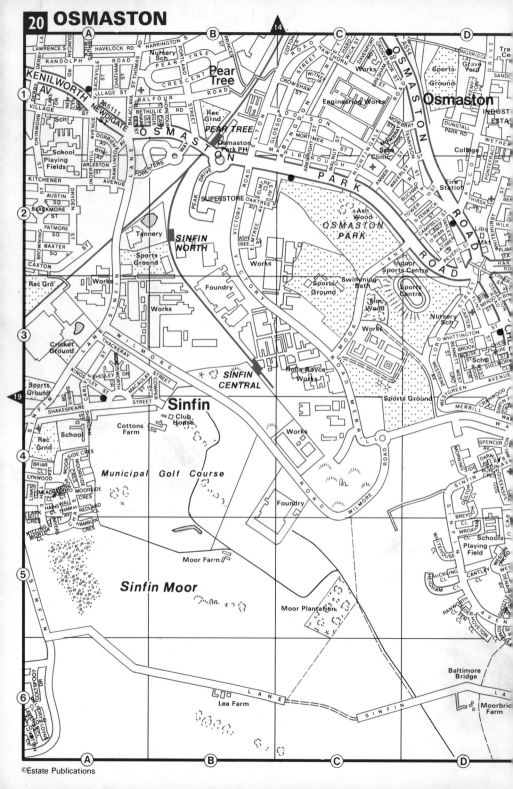

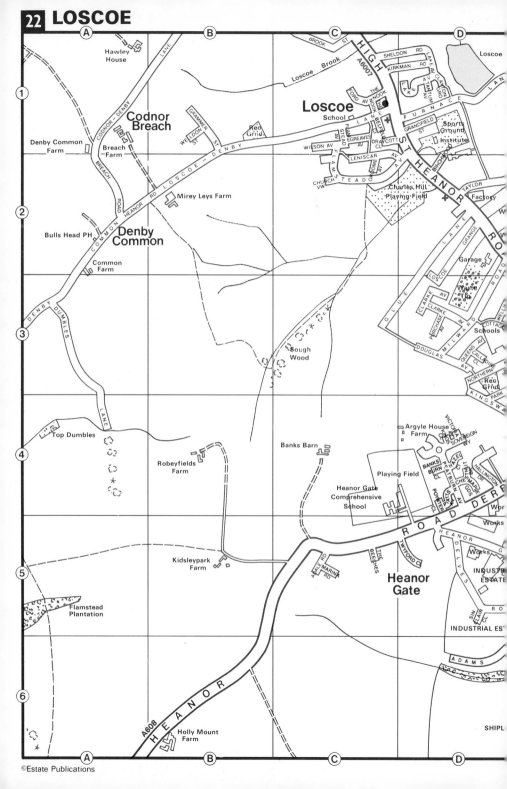

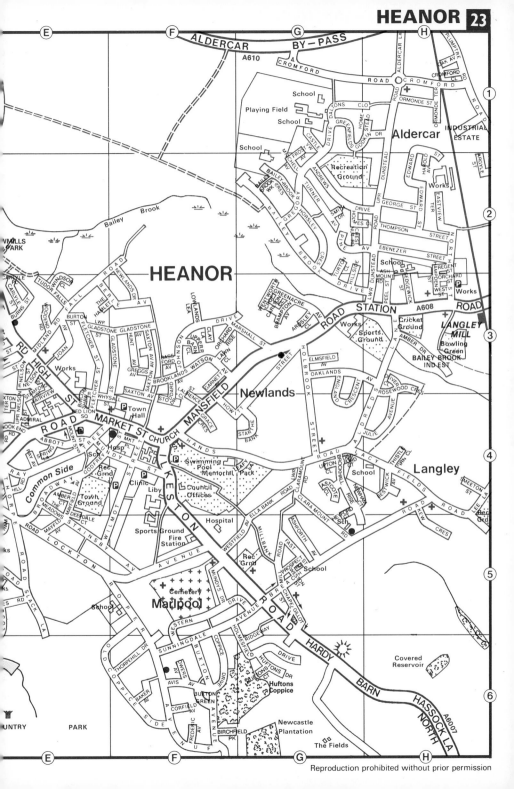

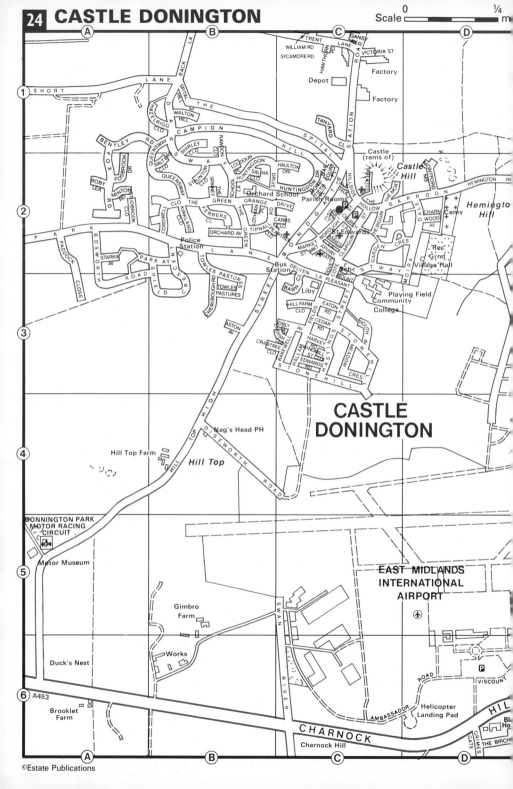

Scale 0 ¼ m

CASTLE DONINGTON

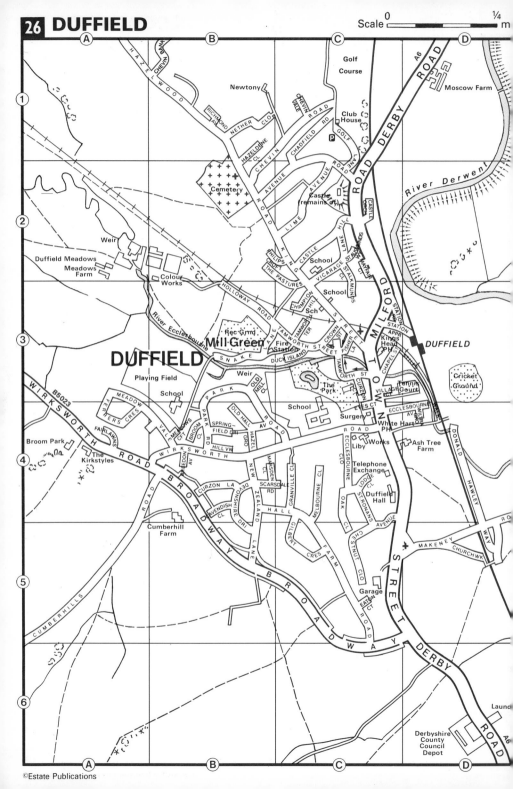

Scale 0 ¼ m

A   B   C   D

DUFFIELD

Golf Course
Newtony
Moscow Farm
Club House
Cemetery
Castle (remains of)
River Derwent
Weir
Duffield Meadows
Meadows Farm
Colour Works
School
School
DUFFIELD
River Ecclesbourne
Rec Grnd
Mill Green
Fire Station
Duck Island
Kings Head PH
Cricket Ground
Playing Field
School
Weir
The Park
Surgery
White Hart PH
Tennis Court
Village
Broom Park
The Kirkstyles
Spring Field
Old Hall
Hazel
Works
Ash Tree Farm
Liby
Telephone Exchange
Duffield Hall
Cumberhill Farm
Scarsdale
Garage
Makeney Church Wk
WIRKSWORTH ROAD
B5023
BROADWAY
CUMBERHILLS
DERBY ROAD
STREET
MILFORD
Derbyshire County Council Depot
Laund
DERBY ROAD

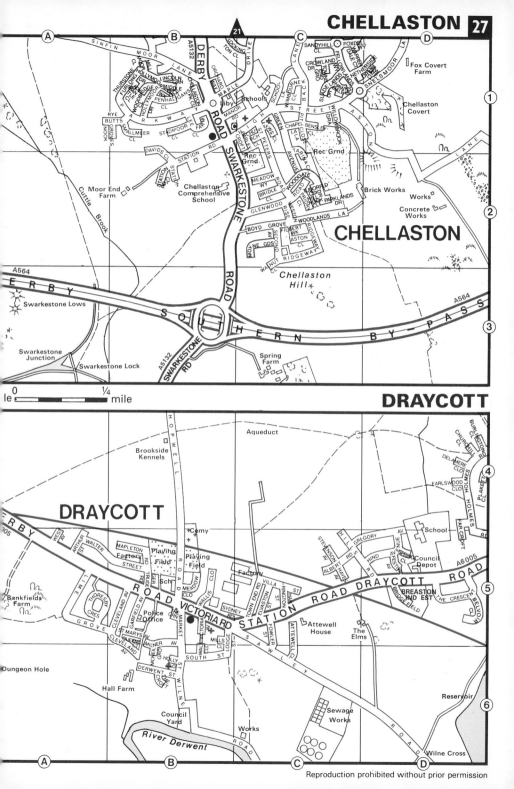

DRAYCOTT

DRAYCOTT

CHELLASTON

A - Z INDEX TO STREETS
with Postcodes

The Index includes some names for which there is insufficient space on the maps. These names are preceded by an * and are followed by the nearest adjoining thoroughfare.

DERBY

Abbey Hill. DE22 9 F2
Abbey Hill Rd. DE22 8 D3
Abbey La. DE22 9 F4
Abbey St. DE22 6 B6
Abbey Yd. DE22 9 F4
Abbeyfields Clo. DE22 9 F4
Abbot Clo. DE21 10 B3
*Abbot Mews,
  New Rd. DE22 9 F4
Abbots Barn Clo. DE22 6 B5
Aberdare Clo. DE21 11 F3
Abingdon St. DE24 20 C1
Abney Clo. DE3 12 C5
Acacia Av. DE3 12 B6
Acorn Clo. DE24 21 E5
Acorn Way. DE21 11 F4
Acton Rd. DE22 12 D1
Addison Rd. DE24 20 C1
Adelaide Clo. DE3 12 C3
Adler Ct. DE1 6 D1
Adrian St. DE24 29 D2
Agard St. DE1 6 A2
Aimploy Clo. DE23 14 B6
Ainley Clo. DE24 21 F2
Ainsworth Dri. DE23 19 G2
Airedale Walk. DE24 21 H2
Albany Rd. DE22 13 F4
Albemarle Rd. DE21 16 A1
Albert Cres. DE21 15 H3
Albert Rd. DE21 15 G3
Albert St. DE1 6 C4
Albion St. DE1 6 C4
Albrighton Av. DE24 19 F6
Alder Clo. DE21 10 C3
Alder Walk. DE21 6 C6
Alderfen Clo. DE24 20 D5
*Alderly Ct, Winchcombe
  Way. DE21 11 E3
Aldersgate. DE22 12 D1
Aldersley Clo. DE65 18 A6
Aldwick Clo. DE3 12 A5
Aldwych. DE22 13 E1
Alexandra Gdns. DE23 14 C5
Alexandre Clo. DE22 19 G2
Alfreton Rd. DE21 10 A3
Alice St. DE1 6 D2
Alison Clo. DE21 10 D6
All Saints Ct. DE3 12 B6
Allan Av. DE23 18 C1
Allen St. DE24 20 D3
Allestree Clo. DE24 21 E1
Allestree La. DE22 8 D4
Allestree St. DE24 21 E1
Alma Heights. DE3 12 C5
Alma St. DE22 6 A4
Almond St. DE23 14 B5
Alsager Clo. DE21 11 E5
Alstonfield Dri. DE22 9 E4
Alton Clo. DE22 8 D3
Alum Clo. DE24 21 H2
Alvaston St. DE24 21 G1
Alverton Clo. DE3 12 A6
Alwards Clo. DE24 21 F2
Amber Rd. DE22 8 D4
Amber St. DE24 20 C2
Amberley Dri. DE24 19 H3
Ambrose St. DE23 14 B5
Ambrose Ter. DE22 13 H2
Amen Alley. DE1 6 C3
Amesbury La. DE21 10 C4
Amy St. DE22 13 G4
*Anchor Fold,
  Madeley St. DE24 14 C5
Anderson St. DE21 21 F2
Andrew Clo. DE23 18 C1
Anglers La. DE21 16 C4
Anglesey St. DE21 15 H3
Anne Potter Clo. DE72 17 G2
Anstey Ct. DE21 10 D4
Anthony Cres. DE24 21 F3
Anthony Dri. DE24 21 F3

Appian Way. DE24 21 H3
Appleby Ct. DE22 13 H4
Applecross Ct. DE24 19 G5
Appledore Dri. DE21 11 E4
Applegate Clo. DE21 11 E3
Appleton Clo. DE21 15 G1
Appletree Clo. DE72 17 G6
Arbor Clo. DE22 6 A5
Arboretum Sq. DE23 14 C4
Arboretum St. DE23 14 C4
Archer St. DE24 15 E5
Arden Clo. DE23 13 G5
Ardleigh Clo. DE3 18 B1
Argyle St. DE22 13 H4
Argyll Clo. DE21 16 D3
Arkendale Walk. DE24 21 H2
Arkle Grn. DE24 19 F4
Arkwright St. DE24 20 C2
Arleston La. DE24 19 G5
Arleston St. DE23 20 A2
Arlington Dri. DE24 21 E3
Arlington Rd. DE23 12 A6
*Armscote Clo, Charingworth
  Rd. DE21 11 E4
Arnhem Ter. DE21 16 C4
Arnold St. DE22 13 G2
Arran Clo. DE24 19 G5
Arreton Ct. DE24 21 H4
Arridge Rd. DE21 15 F1
*Arthur Ct,
  Malcolm St. DE23 14 C5
Arthur Hind Clo. DE22 9 E6
Arthur St. DE1 6 B1
Arundel Av. DE3 12 C5
Arundel Dri. DE21 16 D3
Arundel St. DE22 13 G4
Ascot Dri. DE24 20 D2
Ash Clo. DE22 9 E4
Ash Tree Clo. DE21 10 C2
*Ashbourne Ct, Uttoxeter
  Old Rd. DE1 13 G3
Ashbourne Rd. DE22 13 F1
Ashbrook Av. DE72 17 F5
Ashbrook Clo. DE22 8 C3
Ashby St. DE24 21 E1
Ashcombe Gdns. DE21 11 E4
Ashcroft Clo. DE24 21 F2
Ashe Pl. DE23 13 H6
Ashfield Av. DE21 10 C5
Ashgrove Ct. DE21 11 F4
Ashleigh Dri. DE73 21 F6
Ashley St. DE22 13 F2
Ashlyn Rd. DE21 14 D2
Ashmeadow. DE22 13 E1
Ashopton Av. DE23 19 H1
Ashovers Clo. DE21 10 C5
*Ashover Rd,
  Chaddesden. DE21 10 C5
Ashton Clo. DE3 12 A4
Ashtree Av. DE24 20 B2
Ashwater Clo. DE24 19 H6
Ashworth Av. DE21 15 F3
Askerfield Av. DE22 8 C2
Aspen Dri. DE21 16 A3
Asterdale Vw. DE21 16 D3
Aston Rd. DE23 19 F5
Astorville Park Rd. DE73 21 F5
Atchison Gdns. DE21 16 A1
Atherfield Walk. DE24 21 H3
Athlone Clo. DE21 10 B5
Athol Clo. DE23 19 G4
Atlow Rd. DE21 10 C6
Attlebridge Clo. DE21 10 B5
*Atworth Gro,
  Bridgerass Rd. DE23 18 D2
Auckland Clo. DE3 12 C4
Audrey Dri. DE21 11 E5
Augusta St. DE23 14 B5
Aults Clo. DE65 18 A6
Austen Av. DE23 19 E1
Austin Sq. DE23 19 H2
Autumn Gro. DE21 15 G3
Averham Clo. DE21 11 E5
Aviemore Way. DE24 19 G4
Avocet Ct. DE24 19 G4
Avon Clo. DE21 15 G6
Avondale Rd. DE21 6 B6
Avonmouth Dri. DE24 21 E1
Aycliffe Gdns. DE21 21 E4

Aylesbury Av. DE21 10 C6
Ayre Clo. DE21 16 C3
Babbacombe Clo. DE24 21 H2
Babington La. DE1 6 C5
Back La. DE73 21 F6
Back Sitwell St. DE1 6 C5
Badger Clo. DE21 16 D1
Bagshaw St. DE24 21 E1
Bailey St. DE23 14 B4
Bainbridge St. DE23 14 B5
Bains Dri. DE72 17 G6
Bakeacre La. DE65 18 B6
Bakehouse La. DE72 17 F5
Baker St. DE24 21 E1
Bakers La. DE1 6 B5
Bakewell Clo. DE3 12 B4
Bakewell St. DE22 6 A4
Balaclava Rd. DE23 20 A1
Balfour Rd. DE23 20 A1
Balham Walk. DE22 12 D1
Ballards Way. DE72 17 G6
Ballater Clo. DE24 19 H4
Balleny Clo. DE21 11 E4
Balmoral Clo. DE23 13 E5
Balmoral Rd. DE22 17 F6
*Balness Ct, Tobermory
  Way. DE24 19 G5
Bamburgh Clo. DE21 16 C3
Bamford Av. DE23 19 H1
Bancroft Dri. DE22 8 D2
Bangor St. DE21 10 C6
Bank Side. DE22 9 E4
Bank View Rd. DE22 9 F5
Bankfield Dri. DE21 16 D3
Bankholmes Clo. DE24 19 G6
Bannels Av. DE23 19 E2
Banwell Clo. DE23 12 A4
*Barcheston Clo, Charingworth
  Rd. DE21 11 E4
Barden Dri. DE22 9 F3
Bare La. DE72 17 F3
Barker Clo. DE3 12 C6
Barleycorn Clo. DE21 11 F3
Barlow St. DE1 14 D4
Barn Clo. DE65 18 B5
Barnard Rd. DE21 10 B4
Barnes Grn. DE22 13 E1
*Barnstaple Clo, Countisbury
  Dri. DE21 10 D4
Barnwood Clo. DE3 12 A5
Baron Clo. DE21 11 G3
Barrett St. DE24 21 F2
Barrie Dri. DE24 20 A4
Barrons Way. DE72 17 F6
Barton Clo. DE21 16 D2
Basildon Clo. DE24 21 E4
Baslow Dri. DE22 9 F3
Bass St. DE22 13 F2
Bassingham Clo. DE21 11 E4
Bateman St. DE23 14 D5
Bath Rd. DE3 12 C5
Bath St. DE1 6 C1
Baverstock Dri. DE73 21 F5
Baxter Sq. DE23 19 H2
Bayleaf Cres. DE21 11 E3
Bayswater Clo. DE22 12 D2
Beardmore Clo. DE21 10 C4
Beatty St. DE24 21 E1
*Beaufort Ct Ind Est,
  Mansfield Rd. DE1 9 H5
Beaufort Rd. DE24 19 F6
Beaufort St. DE21 10 B5
Beaumaris Ct. DE21 16 D2
Beaumont Walk. DE23 19 H2
Beaureper Av. DE22 8 D2
Becher St. DE23 14 C6
Beckenham Way. DE22 13 E1
Becket St. DE1 6 B4
Becket Well La. DE1 6 B4
Beckett Clo. DE24 21 F1
Bedford Clo. DE22 13 G4
Bedford St. DE22 13 G3
Beech Av,
  Alvaston. DE24 20 C4
Beech Av,
  Borrowash. DE72 17 F4
Beech Clo. DE21 16 C3
Beech Croft. DE21 10 B2
Beech Delve. DE65 18 B6
Beech Dri. DE22 9 F5

Beech Gdns. DE24 21 G1
Beech Walk. DE23 13 G6
Beeches Av. DE21 16 B3
Beechley Dri. DE21 11 E4
Beechwood Cres. DE23 13 F6
Beeley Clo,
  Allestree. DE22 8 D4
Beeley Clo,
  Chaddesden. DE21 10 D4
Belfast Walk. DE21 15 H3
Belfry Clo. DE3 12 D6
Belgrave St. DE23 14 B4
Bellingham Ct. DE22 8 C4
Belmont Dri. ED72 17 F5
Belmont Rd. DE3 12 B3
Belper Rd. DE1 9 F6
Belsize Clo. DE22 12 D2
Belvedere Clo. DE3 12 B4
Belvoir St. DE23 14 A5
Bembridge Dri. DE24 21 H3
Bemrose Mews. DE22 13 F4
Bemrose Rd. DE24 20 D2
Bendall Grn. DE23 19 F3
Benmore Clo. DE21 11 E3
Bennett St. DE24 20 D3
Benson St. DE24 21 E2
Bentley St. DE24 21 E2
Beresford Dri. DE21 16 D4
Berkley Clo. DE23 19 G1
Berkshire St. DE21 10 B6
Berry Park Clo. DE22 9 E4
Berrysford Clo. DE21 15 F3
Berwick Av. DE21 10 B6
Berwick Av. DE24 19 F5
Berwick Clo. DE24 21 G4
Besthorpe Clo. DE21 11 E5
*Betjeman Sq, Wordsworth
  Dri. DE24 20 A3
Bethulie Rd. DE23 20 A1
Beverley St. DE24 15 E5
Bewdley Clo. DE73 21 F5
Bexhill Walk. DE21 10 B4
Bicester Av. DE24 19 F6
*Bickley Moss,
  Rosemoor La. DE21 11 E4
Bideford Clo. DE23 19 G3
Bingham St. DE23 20 D3
Binscombe La. DE21 10 C3
Birch Clo. DE21 17 E2
Birch View Ct. DE22 6 A1
Birches Rd. DE22 8 D2
Birchfield Clo. DE73 21 F6
Birchover Rise. DE21 10 D4
Birchover Way. DE22 8 D4
Birchwood Av. DE72 19 F3
Birdcage Walk. DE22 12 D2
Birdwood St. DE24 14 A6
Birkdale Clo. DE3 12 D5
Biscay Ct. DE21 11 F3
Bishops Dri. DE21 10 B3
Blaby Clo. DE23 19 G3
Blackmore St. DE23 19 H2
Blackmount Ct. DE24 19 G5
Blackthorn Clo. DE21 10 C3
Blagreaves Av. DE23 19 F3
Blagreaves La. DE23 19 F1
Blakebrook Dri. DE73 21 F5
Blakeney Clo. DE21 11 F4
Blandford Clo. DE24 21 H3
Blankney Clo. DE24 19 G6
Blencathra Dri. DE3 12 C6
Blenheim Dri. DE22 8 D2
Blithfield Gdns. DE73 21 F6
Bloomfield Clo. DE1 14 C4
Bloomfield St. DE1 14 D4
Bluebell Clo. DE24 19 F6
Bluebird Clo. DE24 19 G4
Blyth Pl. DE21 10 B4
Boden St. DE23 14 C5
Bodmin Clo. DE24 19 G5
Bodmin Grn. DE24 21 G3
Bold La. DE1 6 B3
Bonchurch Clo. DE24 21 H3
Bonnyrigg Dri. DE21 10 D4
Bonsall Av. DE23 13 G6
Bonsall Dri. DE3 12 B4
Booth St. DE24 20 D4
Border Cres. DE24 21 G4
Borrow Fields. DE72 17 F6
Borrowash By-Pass.
  DE21 16 D1
Borrowash Rd. DE21 16 D3
Borrowfield Rd. DE21 16 C4

Boscastle Rd. DE24 21 G
Boston Clo. DE21 16
Boswell Sq. DE23 19
Bosworth Av. DE23 19 C
Boulton Dri. DE24 21
Boulton La. DE24 21
Boundary Rd. DE22 13 C
Bourne St. DE1 6
Bowbridge Av. DE21 19
Bower St. DE24 21
Bowland Clo. DE3 12
Bowlees Ct. DE23 18
Bowmer Rd. DE24 15
Boxmore Clo. DE23 18
Boyer St. DE22 6
*Boyer Walk,
  Boyer St. DE22 6
Boylestone Rd. DE23 19
Brackens Av. DE24 21
Brackens La. DE24 21
Brackensdale Av. DE22 13
Brackley Dri. DE21 16
Bracknell Dri. DE24 21
Bradbourne Clo. DE22 13
Bradbury Clo. DE72 17
Bradgate Ct. DE23 19
Brading Clo. DE24 21
Bradley St. DE22 9
Bradshaw Way. DE1 6
Bradwell Clo. DE3 12
Braemar Clo. DE24 19
Brailsford Rd. DE21 10
Braintree Clo. DE21 10
Braithwell Clo. DE22 9
Bramble St. DE1 6
*Brambleberry Ct, Cherrybro
  Dri. DE21 11
Bramfield Av. DE22 13
Bramfield Ct. DE22 13
Bramley Clo. DE21 11
Brampton Clo. DE3 12
Brandelhow Ct. DE21 11
Branksome Av. DE24 21
Brassington Rd. DE21 10
Brayfield Av. DE23 19
Brayfield Rd. DE23 13
Brecon Clo. DE21 16
Breedon Av. DE23 19
Breedon Hill Rd. DE23 14
Brentford Dri. DE22 13
Bretby Sq. DE23 19
Bretton Av. DE21 19
Breydon Clo. DE24 20
Briar Clo. DE72 17
Briar Clo. DE21 16
Briar Lea Clo. DE24 19
Briars Gate. DE22 8
Briars La. DE23 19
Briarwood Way. DE23 19
Brick Row. DE1
Brick St. DE1 13
Bridge Gate. DE1 6
Bridge St. DE1 6
*Bridgend Ct, Leominster
  Dri. DE21 11
Bridgeness Rd. DE23 18
Bridgeport Rd. DE21 16
Bridgwater Dri. DE24 21
Brierfield Way. DE3 12
Brigden Av. DE24 20
Brighstone Clo. DE24 19
Bright St. DE22 13
Brighton Rd. DE24 21
Brigmor Walk. DE22 13
Brindley Clo. DE24 19
*Brindley Ct,
  Evans St. DE24 21
Brisbane Rd. DE24 19
Briset Clo. DE24 19
Bristol Dri. DE24 19
Britannia Ct. DE21 19
Broadbank. DE22 8
*Broadleaf Clo, Spindletree
  Dri. DE21 11
Broadway Park Clo.
  DE22 8
Broadstone Clo. DE21 10
Broadway. DE21 16
Brockley. DE21 16
Bromley St. DE22 9
Brompton Clo. DE22 13
Bromyard Dri. DE73 21

28

nte Pl. DE23 19 E1
ok Clo,
urley La. DE22 8 C2
ok Clo,
ndern. DE65 18 B6
ok Gdns. DE22 6 A1
ok Clo. DE72 17 F6
ok St. DE1 6 A2
ok Walk. DE1 6 A2
okfield Av. DE21 11 E6
okfield Av. DE23 19 G2
okfields Dri. DE21 10 B2
okhouse St. DE24 20 D3
oklands Dri. DE23 19 F1
okside Clo. DE22 13 G1
okside Rd. DE21 10 B2
om Clo. DE73 21 E6
om Clo. DE24 19 G6
omhill Clo. DE3 12 B4
ugh St. DE22 13 G2
ughton Av. DE23 13 G6
wning Circle. DE23 19 H2
wning St. DE23 19 H1
nswick St. DE23 14 B6
nswood Clo. DE21 16 C2
nton Clo. DE3 12 A6
ony Clo. DE21 10 D4
han St. DE24 20 D2
hanan St. DE1 6 C1
kingham Av. DE21 10 B6
kland Clo. DE22 13 H2
kminster Clo. DE21 10 D3
er St. DE23 13 H5
ting Clo. DE3 13 E4
oage Pl. DE24 21 E2
dock Clo. DE21 10 C3
ghley Clo. DE73 21 E6
ghley Way. DE23 18 C3
leigh Dri. DE22 9 F6
lington Rd. DE22 12 C2
lington Way. DE22 12 B6
naby St. DE24 15 F6
nage Ct. DE22 6 A5
nham Dri. DE3 12 A5
ns Clo. DE23 19 E1
nside Clo. DE24 19 G5
nside Clo. DE3 16 D3
nside St. DE24 21 F1
rowfield Mews.
21 16 D5
ows Walk. DE1 6 C4
on Rd, Derby. DE1 6 A6
on Rd,
ndern. DE65 18 A6
on Rd,
tleover. DE23 13 E6
Walk. DE21 10 B6
ermere Dri. DE22 9 E2
onoak Dri. DE73 21 F5
on Dri. DE21 12 C4
on Rd. DE21 10 D5
eld Clo. DE21 11 F3
g Av. DE23 20 A1
n St. DE23 14 B5

Cardigan St. DE21 10 B6
Cardrona Clo. DE21 10 D4
Carisbrooke Gdns. DE23 19 F3
Carlisle Av. DE23 19 E1
Carlton Av. DE24 20 D5
Carlton Clo. DE24 20 D5
Carlton Gdns. DE24 20 D5
Carlton Rd. DE23 13 G6
Carlyle St. DE24 20 A3
Carnegie St. DE23 20 B1
Carnforth Clo. DE3 12 C6
Carnoustie Clo. DE3 12 D5
Carol Cres. DE21 15 F3
Caroline Clo. DE24 21 H2
Carrington St. DE1 6 D5
Carron Clo. DE24 19 G4
Carsington Cres. DE22 8 D5
Carsington Mews. DE22 9 E5
Carson Rd. DE21 16 A1
Carter St. DE24 20 D3
Cascade Gro. DE23 18 D1
Casson Av. DE24 21 F2
Castings Rd. DE21 14 C6
Castle Croft. DE21 21 H4
Castle Hill. DE65 18 B6
Castle Shaw Dri. DE24 18 C2
Castle St. DE1 6 D5
Castle Walk. DE1 6 D4
Castle Ward Ind Est. DE1 14 C3
Castlecraig Ct. DE24 19 G6
Castleton Av. DE23 19 H1
Cathedral Pl. DE1 6 C2
Cathedral Rd. DE1 6 B2
Cathedral Vw. DE22 13 G5
Catherine St. DE23 14 C5
Catterick Dri. DE3 12 A6
Causeway. DE22 9 E3
Cavan Dri. DE21 15 H3
Cavendish Av. DE22 9 E3
Cavendish Ct. DE1 6 B2
Cavendish St. DE1 6 A3
Cavendish Way. DE3 12 C5
Caversfield Clo. DE23 18 D1
Caxton St. DE23 19 G2
Cecil St. DE22 13 G2
Cedar Dri. DE72 17 G3
Cedar St. DE22 9 E4
Celandine Clo. DE21 10 D4
Celanese Rd. DE21 16 B4
Central Av. DE72 17 F6
Centre Ct. DE1 14 D4
Centurion Walk. DE1 9 G6
Chaddesden La. DE21 15 G2
Chaddesden Lane End.
DE21 15 G2
Chaddesden Park Rd.
DE21 15 F2
Chadwick Av. DE24 21 E3
Chaffinch Clo. DE21 16 D1
Chain La. DE23 13 E6
Chalfont Sq. DE21 11 F4
Chalkley Clo. DE24 21 E1
Challis Av. DE21 15 H1
Chambers St. DE24 15 F6
Chancel Pl. DE22 6 A6
Chancery La. DE22 13 E2
Chandlers Ford. DE21 10 C4
Chandos St. DE21 13 G2
Chandres Ct. DE22 9 E2
Chantry Clo. DE3 12 B6
Chapel La,
Cherrytree Hill. DE21 15 G1
Chapel La, Derby. DE1 14 C4
Chapel La,
Spondon. DE21 16 C2
Chapel Pl. DE1 6 C5
Chapel Row. DE72 17 F5
Chapel St, Derby. DE1 6 B2
Chapel St,
Spondon. DE21 16 C3
*Chapelside,
Strathaven. DE21 16 C3
Chapman Av. DE24 21 G2
Chapter Clo. DE21 10 B3
Charing Clo. DE1 6 D1
Charingworth Rd. DE21 11 E4
Chariot Clo. DE24 21 H3
Charlbury Clo. DE23 18 B1
Charles Av. DE21 16 C2
Charleston Dri. DE22 8 D2
Charleston Rd. DE21 16 A2
Charlotte St. DE23 14 B5
Charnwood Av. DE22 17 G5
Charnwood Av. DE23 19 G3
Charnwood St. DE1 6 C6
Charnwood Walk. DE22 9 F4
Charterhouse Clo. DE1 10 C5
Charterstone La. DE22 9 E2
Chartwell Dri. DE21 14 D2
Chatham St. DE23 20 A1

Chatsworth Av. DE22 9 E3
Chatsworth Ct. DE24 20 A4
Chatsworth Dri. DE3 12 C5
Chatsworth St. DE23 14 A6
Chatteris Dri. DE21 10 B6
Cheadle Clo. DE23 13 E6
Cheam Clo. DE24 12 C2
Cheapside. DE1 6 B3
Chedworth Dri. DE24 21 H3
Chellaston Rd. DE24 20 D3
Chelmarsh Clo. DE72 21 F5
Chelmorton Pl. DE21 10 D5
Chelmsford Clo. DE3 14 B4
Chelsea Clo. DE22 12 C2
Chelwood Rd. DE73 21 E6
Chequers La. DE21 15 E2
Chequers Rd. DE21 15 E2
Cheriton Gdns. DE23 18 C2
Cherry Tree Mews.
DE21 16 A3
Cherrybrook Dri. DE21 11 E3
Chertsey Rd. DE3 12 A5
Chesapeake Rd. DE21 16 A2
Cheshire St. DE24 20 D3
Chester Av. DE22 9 G1
Chester Ct. DE21 11 E4
Chester Green Rd. DE1 9 G6
Chesterford St. DE23 18 C2
Chesterton Av. DE23 19 G2
Chesterton Rd. DE21 16 D2
Chestnut Av. DE3 12 B4
Chestnut Av. DE23 14 B5
Chestnut Av. DE73 21 E5
Chestnut Gro. DE72 17 F4
Cheveley Ct. DE21 10 B5
Cheverton Clo. DE21 21 H4
Chevin Av,
Borrowash. DE72 17 F5
Chevin Av,
Mickleover. DE3 12 D5
Chevin Pl. DE1 9 F6
Chevin Rd. DE1 9 F6
Cheviot St. DE22 13 F2
Cheyenne Gdns. DE21 16 A2
Cheyne Walk. DE22 13 F1
Chilston Dri. DE3 12 A4
Chime Clo. DE21 10 C4
Chingford Ct. DE22 13 E2
Chinley Rd. DE21 10 D5
Chiswick Clo. DE22 12 D2
*Christchurch Ct,
St Michaels La. DE1 6 C2
Church Hill. DE21 16 C3
Church Hill Ter. DE21 16 C3
Church La,
Allestree. DE22 9 E3
Church La,
Breadsall. DE21 10 B2
Church La,
Cherrytree Hill. DE21 15 G1
Church La,
Markeaton. DE22 8 A6
Church Lane Nth. DE22 9 F3
Church Mews. DE21 16 C3
Church Rd. DE22 8 C2
Church St. DE24 21 H2
Church St,
Littleover. DE23 13 F6
Church St. DE72 17 G3
Church St,
Rose Hill. DE23 14 B5
Church St. DE21 16 C3
Church Walk. DE22 9 F2
Churchdown Ct. DE21 11 E3
Churchside Walk. DE22 13 G4
City Rd. DE1 6 C1
Clarence Rd. DE23 14 A6
Clarke St. DE1 6 D1
Cleveland Av. DE21 15 H3
Clifford St. DE24 15 E5
Clifton Clo. DE3 12 C4
Clifton Dri. DE3 8 D3
Clifton St. DE1 14 D4
Clinton St. DE21 15 E2
Clipstone Gdns. DE21 11 F4
Clock Way. DE21 16 D4
*Clock Yard,
Vernon St. DE1 13 H2
Cloudwood Clo. DE23 13 E6
Clover Clo. DE21 16 D3
Cloverdale Dri. DE24 19 H6
Cloverslade. DE65 18 A6
Clumber Ter. DE21 15 E5
Cobden St. DE23 13 G2
Cobham Clo. DE24 19 F5
Cobthorn Pl. DE22 8 D2
Coburn Pl. DE1 6 B3
Cockayne St Nth. DE24 21 E2
Cockayne St Sth. DE24 21 E3

Codbeck Clo. DE24 21 H2
Coke St. DE22 13 G3
Coldstream Walk. DE24 19 G4
Cole La. DE72 17 G4
Coleman St. DE24 21 E2
Coleraine Clo. DE21 15 H3
Coleridge St. DE23 19 H3
College Mews. DE1 13 G3
College Pl. DE1 6 C2
Collingham Gdns. DE22 12 D2
Collier La. DE72 17 F4
Collis Clo. DE24 21 E2
Collumbell Av. DE72 17 G2
Colombo St. DE23 14 C6
Coltsfoot Dri. DE24 19 H6
Columbine Clo. DE21 10 D4
Colvile St. DE22 13 G2
Colwell Dri. DE24 21 H4
Colwyn Av. DE23 13 G6
Colyear St. DE1 6 B4
Comfrey Clo. DE23 18 D2
Commerce St. DE1 15 F6
Common Piece La.
DE65 18 B6
Compton Clo. DE24 21 H3
Coniston Av. DE21 16 C2
Coniston Cres. DE21 10 B4
Connaught Rd. DE22 13 F4
Consett Clo. DE21 10 B5
Consort Gdns. DE21 11 F2
Constable Av. DE23 13 F5
Constable Dri. DE23 13 F5
Constable La. DE23 13 F5
Conway Av. DE72 17 G5
Cookham Clo. DE3 12 A5
Cooper St. DE22 13 F2
Cooperative St. DE23 14 B5
Coopers Clo. DE72 17 G6
*Cope Clo, Wordsworth Dri.
DE24 20 A3
Copecastle Sq. DE1 6 D4
Copeland St. DE1 6 D4
Copes Way. DE21 11 E5
Coppice Clo. DE22 9 F4
Corbel Clo. DE21 10 B4
Corbridge Gro. DE21 18 D2
Corby Clo. DE24 21 F3
Corden Av. DE3 12 D5
Corden St. DE23 14 B5
Cordville Clo. DE21 16 A3
Corfe Clo. DE23 19 F2
Coriander Gdns. DE23 19 F4
Corinium Clo. DE21 21 H3
Corn Market. DE1 6 C3
Cornflower Dri. DE21 11 E3
Cornhill. DE22 9 E2
Cornwall Rd. DE21 15 E1
Coronation Av. DE24 21 G3
Coronation St. DE23 14 C6
Coronet Ct. DE21 11 G3
Corporation St. DE1 6 C3
Cotswold Clo. DE23 9 F1
Cottisford Clo. DE21 19 E1
Cotton Brook Rd. DE23 14 C6
Cotton La. DE24 14 D6
Countisbury Dri. DE21 10 C4
Courtland Dri. DE24 21 G2
Courtland Gdns. DE24 21 G2
Coverdale Walk. DE24 21 H2
Cowdray Clo. DE21 19 G6
Cowley St. DE1 13 H1
Cowper St. DE24 20 B3
Cowsley Rd. DE21 10 B6
Coxgreen Ct. DE23 18 D2
Coxon St. DE21 16 C2
Crabtree Clo. DE22 8 C2
Crabtree Hill. DE21 8 C2
Craddock Av. DE21 16 C4
Craiglee Ct. DE24 19 G5
Cranberry Gro. DE23 18 D2
Cranmer Rd. DE21 14 D2
Cranwood Clo. DE24 20 D4
Crawley Rd. DE24 21 F3
Crayford Rd. DE24 21 F3
Crecy Clo. DE22 13 F4
*Cressbrook Way,
Smalley Dri. DE21 11 E3
Crew St. DE23 14 B6
Crewton Way. DE24 21 E2
Crich Av. DE23 13 F5
Crich Circle. DE23 13 F5
*Cricketers Ct, Taverners
Cres. DE23 19 F1
Cricklewood Rd. DE21 13 E1
Cringle Mews. DE21 10 C4
Croft Clo,
Ockbrook. DE72 17 F3
Croft Clo,
Spondon. DE21 16 D2

Croft La. DE21 10 B3
*Crofters Ct,
Dunsmore Dri. DE21 10 C4
Cromarty Clo. DE24 19 G4
Cromer Clo. DE3 12 A6
Cromford Clo. DE3 12 B4
Cromford Rd. DE21 10 D6
Crompton St. DE1 6 B4
Cromwell Av. DE65 18 B6
Cromwell Rd. DE23 14 B5
Cropton Clo. DE24 21 H2
Crosby St. DE22 13 G4
Cross Clo. DE23 19 F1
Cross Close Walk. DE23 19 F1
Cross St. DE22 13 G2
Crossdale Gro. DE21 11 F3
Crossley St. DE72 17 E5
Crown Mews. DE22 13 H4
Crown St. DE22 6 A6
Crown Walk. DE1 6 C4
Crowshaw St. DE24 20 C1
Croydon Walk. DE22 12 D1
Cubley Walk. DE23 19 F3
Cuckmere Clo. DE22 9 G1
Cullen Way. DE22 19 H6
*Culworth Ct, Charingworth
Rd. DE21 11 E4
Cumberland Av. DE21 15 E1
Cumberland Cres. DE72 17 E5
Cumbria Walk. DE3 12 A6
Cummings St. DE23 14 B5
Curborough Dri. DE24 21 H3
Curlew Clo. DE2 19 G4
Curzon Clo. DE22 8 C2
Curzon Ct. DE3 12 B6
Curzon La. DE24 21 F1
Curzon Rd. DE21 10 D6
Curzon St. DE1 6 A4
Cut La. DE22 9 G6
Cuttlebrook Clo. DE23 19 E2
Cypress Walk. DE21 16 A3
Dahlia Dri. DE21 11 F3
Dairy House Rd. DE23 14 C6
Dalbury Walk. DE23 19 F3
Dale Rd. DE24 21 G2
Dale Rd. DE21 14 B5
Dale Rd. DE21 16 D2
Dalkeith Av. DE24 21 E3
Dalton Av. DE22 13 F4
Danebridge Cres. DE21 11 E4
Darby St. DE23 14 B5
Darley Abbey Dri. DE22 9 F4
Darley Gro. DE22 9 F5
Darley La. DE1 6 B1
Darley Park Dri. DE22 9 F5
Darley Park Rd. DE22 9 F5
Darley St. DE22 9 F4
Dartford Pl. DE24 21 F3
Darwin Av. DE24 20 D4
Darwin Pl. DE1 6 D3
Darwin Rd. DE3 12 C4
Darwin Sq. DE1 6 C4
Dashwood St. DE23 14 B4
Datchet Clo. DE23 19 E1
Davenport Rd. DE24 20 C1
Daventry Clo. DE3 12 A4
Dawlish Ct. DE24 21 H1
Dawsmere Clo. DE21 10 B5
Daylesford Clo. DE23 18 D1
Dayton Clo. DE21 16 A2
Deacon Clo. DE21 10 C3
Deadmans La. DE24 15 E5
Dean Clo. DE23 13 E5
Dean St. DE22 13 G4
Deans Dri. DE72 17 F5
Deborah Dri. DE21 11 E6
Dee Clo. DE24 19 G5
Deep Dale La. DE24 19 H6
Deepdale Av. DE72 17 G5
Deepdale Rd. DE21 16 D4
Deer Park View. DE21 16 D1
Degge St. DE1 6 C4
Dein Court Clo. DE21 11 E5
Delamere Clo. DE21 11 E5
Denarth Av. DE24 20 D5
Denbigh St. DE21 10 C6
Denison Gdns. DE21 11 E3
Dennis Clo. DE23 18 C1
Denstone Dri. DE24 21 F4
Dentdale Ct. DE24 21 H2
Denver Rd. DE3 12 B4
Depot St. DE23 14 C5
Derby La. DE23 19 H1
Derby Rd. DE72 17 E5
Derby Rd,
Chaddesden. DE21 11 G3
Derby Rd,
Cherrytree Hill. DE21 15 G3
Derby Rd. DE73 21 E5

Derrington Leys. DE24 21 H2
Derventio Clo. DE1 9 G6
Derwent Av,
Allestree. DE22 9 F2
Derwent Av,
Borrowash. DE72 17 G5
Derwent Clo. DE22 9 G2
Derwent Dri. DE24 19 G6
Derwent Park. DE1 14 D4
Derwent Rise. DE21 16 D3
Derwent Road. DE21 16 B4
Derwent St. DE1 6 C3
Devas Gdns. DE21 16 B2
Devon Clo. DE21 15 E1
Devonshire Av. DE22 9 E3
Devonshire Av. DE72 17 G5
Devonshire Dri. DE3 12 C5
Devonshire Walk. DE1 6 C4
Dexter St. DE23 14 D5
Diamond Rd. DE21 10 D3
Dickens Sq. DE23 19 H2
Dickinson St. DE24 15 E5
Diseworth Clo. DE73 21 F6
Dodburn Ct. DE24 19 G4
Doles La. DE65 18 A5
Dolphin Clo. DE21 17 E1
Donegal Walk. DE21 15 H3
Donington Clo. DE23 19 G3
Donington Dri. DE23 19 G3
Dorchester Av. DE21 10 C6
Dorking Rd. DE22 13 E2
Dorrien Av. DE23 20 A1
Dorset St. DE21 15 E1
Douglas St. DE23 14 C5
Dove Clo. DE3 12 A4
Dovecote Dri. DE72 17 E5
Dovedale Av. DE24 21 H2
Dovedale Rise. DE22 8 D5
Dovedale Road. DE21 16 D4
Dover Ct. DE23 14 B5
Dover St. DE21 14 B5
Doveridge Walk. DE23 19 F3
Dower Clo. DE22 12 C6
Downham Clo. DE3 12 C6
Downing Clo. DE22 12 D2
Downing Rd. DE21 15 E3
Drage St. DE1 13 H1
Draycott Dri. DE21 12 A4
Draycott Rd. DE72 17 G6
Drayton Av. DE22 12 D1
Dresden Clo. DE3 12 A5
Drewry Ct. DE22 13 H3
Drewry La. DE22 6 A4
Dreyfus Clo. DE21 16 D2
Drury Av. DE21 16 C4
Dryden St. DE23 19 H2
Drysdale Rd. DE3 12 B4
Duesbury Clo. DE24 20 D2
Duffield Clo. DE22 9 F2
Duffield Rd. DE1 6 B1
Duke St. DE1 6 C1
Dukeries La. DE21 11 E4
Duluth Av. DE21 15 H1
Dulverton Av. DE24 19 F6
Dulwich Rd. DE22 12 C2
Dunbar Clo. DE24 19 H6
Duncan Rd. DE23 20 A1
Dunedin Clo. DE3 12 C4
*Dunkery Ct, Countisbury
Dri. DE21 10 D4
Dunkirk. DE22 6 A4
Dunoon Clo. DE24 19 G5
Dunsmore Dri. DE21 14 A4
Dunstall Park Rd. DE24 20 D1
Dunton Clo. DE24 14 D3
*Dunvegan Clo,
Lundie Clo. DE24 19 G6
Durham Av. DE21 15 F2
Durley Clo. DE24 21 H2

Ealing Clo. DE24 13 E1
Eardley Clo. DE21 16 A3
Earls Cres. DE21 11 E4
Earlswood Dri. DE3 12 C4
East Av. DE3 9 E4
East Brae Rd. DE23 19 G2
East Clo. DE21 9 G4
East Lawn. DE65 18 B6
East Service Rd. DE24 15 H5
East St. DE1 14 D5
Eastcroft Av. DE23 19 G4
Eastgate. DE21 14 D5
Eastleigh Dri. DE3 12 C5
Eastwood Av. DE23 13 F5
Eastwood Dri. DE23 13 F5
Eaton Av. DE23 9 G1
Eaton Clo. DE22 9 G1
Eaton Ct. DE1 13 H2
Edale Clo. DE24 21 G2

Edale Av. DE23 13 G5
Edale Av. DE3 12 B5
Edale Clo. DE22 8 D5
Edale Dri. DE21 16 D4
Eden Rd. DE21 15 H3
Eden St. DE24 21 G1
Edensor Sq. DE22 6 A5
*Edgbaston Ct,
Pavilion Rd. DE23 19 F1
Edge Hill. DE73 21 F5
Edgelaw Ct. DE24 19 G5
Edgeware Rd. DE22 12 D1
Edinburgh Cres. DE24 20 D4
Edith Wood Clo. DE24 21 G4
Edmund Rd. DE21 16 D4
Edmunds Sq. DE3 18 A1
Ednaston Av. DE23 19 F3
Edward Av. DE21 15 G3
Edward St. DE1 6 B1
Edwinstowe Rd. DE21 11 E4
Eggesford Rd. DE24 19 G6
*Egmanton Clo, Danebridge
Cres. DE21 11 E4
Eland Clo. DE21 17 E2
Eley Walk. DE1 6 B6
Elgin Av. DE23 13 E6
Eliot Rd. DE23 19 E1
Elizabeth Clo. DE21 15 H3
Elkstone Clo. DE21 11 E3
Ellastone Gdns. DE24 21 G2
Ellendale Rd. DE21 16 A1
Ellesmere Av. DE24 15 E5
Elm Cres. DE21 15 H3
Elm Gro. DE22 8 D1
Elm Park Ct. DE22 6 A1
Elm St,
Borrowash. DE72 17 F5
Elm St, Derby. DE1 13 H1
Elms Av. DE23 13 E6
Elms Dri. DE23 13 E6
*Elms Farm Way,
Swanmore Rd. DE23 18 D1
Elms Gdn. DE23 13 E6
Elmtree Av. DE24 20 B2
Elmwood Dri. DE21 10 B4
Elton Rd. DE24 20 B1
Elvaston La. DE24 21 G2
Embankment Clo. DE22 12 D1
Emerald Clo. DE21 10 D3
Emerson Sq. DE21 19 H2
Emmerdale Walk. DE21 10 B4
Empress Rd. DE23 14 A5
Endsleigh Gdns. DE22 12 D1
Enfield Rd. DE22 13 E1
Ennis Clo. DE21 16 A1
Enoch Pine Clo. DE21 16 A3
Epping Clo. DE22 12 C2
Epworth Dri. DE24 21 G4
Esdale Walk. DE24 21 H3
Essex St. DE21 15 E1
Eton St. DE24 15 E6
Etruria Gdns. DE1 6 C1
Ettrick Dri. DE24 19 H6
Etwall Rd. DE3 12 A6
Etwall St. DE22 13 G2
Euston Dri. DE1 6 D1
Evans Av. DE22 9 F1
Evans St. DE24 21 E2
Evanston Gdns. DE21 16 A2
Evelyn Gro. DE21 15 G3
Evergreen Clo. DE21 11 E3
Evesham Clo. DE21 10 C4
Excelsior Av. DE24 21 E2
Exchange St. DE1 6 C4
Exeter Pl. DE1 6 D3
Exeter St. DE1 6 D2

Fairbourne Dri. DE3 12 B3
Fairdene Ct. DE3 14 B5
Faire St. DE22 13 H4
Faires Clo. DE72 17 G6
Fairfax Rd. DE23 14 A5
Fairfield Av. DE72 17 F4
Fairfield Rd. DE23 13 G6
Fairisle Clo. DE21 11 F3
Fairview Clo. DE23 18 D1
Fairway Clo. DE22 8 D3
Fairway Cres. DE22 8 D4
Fairwood Dri. DE24 21 H3
Fallow Rd. DE21 16 D1
Falmouth Rd. DE24 21 H4
Far La. DE72 17 G2
Farley Clo. DE22 13 F5
Farley Rd. DE23 13 G5
Farm Dri. DE24 21 F3
Farm St. DE22 6 A5
Farmhouse Rd. DE24 19 G6
Farmlands La. DE23 19 E2
Farnborough Gdns. DE22 8 D5

Farncombe La. DE21 10 C3
Farndale Ct. DE24 21 H2
Farnham Clo. DE3 12 A6
Farningham Clo. DE21 16 D2
Farnway. DE22 9 E4
Farnworth Rd. DE3 12 B5
Farringdon Clo. DE22 12 C2
Faversham Clo. DE24 21 F3
Fellside. DE21 16 D2
Fenchurch Walk. DE22 13 E1
Fenton Rd. DE3 12 A5
Fenwick St. DE24 20 D2
Fernhill Ct. DE73 21 F5
Fernilee Gdns. DE21 10 D4
Fernwood Clo. DE23 13 F6
Ferrers Way. DE22 9 E4
Field Clo. DE72 17 F4
Field Cres. DE24 21 F3
Field Dri. DE24 21 G4
Field La. DE21 21 G3
Field La. DE21 10 D6
Field Rise. DE23 19 F1
Field View Clo. DE24 21 G4
Fieldgate Dri. DE21 10 C3
Fieldhead Way. DE21 11 E3
Fife St. DE24 15 F6
Filey Walk. DE21 10 B5
Fincham Clo. DE21 10 B5
Finchley Av. DE22 12 D1
Findern Clo. DE22 8 D5
Findern La. DE65 18 A5
Findern St. DE22 13 G2
Finmere Clo. DE23 19 E1
Finningley Dri. DE22 9 E4
Finsbury Av. DE22 13 E2
Finsley Walk. DE23 19 H2
Firs Cres. DE22 9 E2
*Firtree Gro,
Beechley Dri. DE21 11 E4
Fisher St. DE24 20 D3
Fiskerton Way. DE21 11 E5
Five Lamps. DE1 6 A1
Flamstead St. DE24 20 D2
Flat Sq. DE22 9 F4
Fleet St. DE23 14 C5
Flint St. DE24 20 D3
Flood St. DE72 17 F3
Folkestone Dri. DE24 21 F4
Folly Rd. DE22 9 G4
Ford La. DE22 9 G1
Ford St. DE1 6 A3
Fordwells Clo. DE23 18 D1
Foremark Av. DE23 19 G1
Forester St. DE1 6 B5
Foresters Way. DE23 20 A2
Forman St. DE1 6 A4
Forum Clo. DE24 21 H3
Fountains Clo. DE22 9 F2
Fowler Av. DE21 16 B3
Fowler St. DE1 13 H2
Fox Av. DE21 19 F6
Fox St. DE1 6 C1
Foxes Walk. DE21 9 E2
Foxfields Dri. DE21 10 C4
Foxglove Dri. DE21 10 D3
Foxlands Av. DE22 9 E3
Foxley Ct. DE21 11 E2
Foyle Av. DE21 15 G3
*Frampton Gdns, Littlewoodbury
Dri. DE21 18 D2
*Franchise Ct,
Franchise St. DE22 13 G3
Franchise St. DE22 13 G3
Francis St. DE21 15 E2
*Frank Dayton Ct,
Cedar St. DE22 9 E6
Franklyn Dri. DE24 21 F3
Frazer Clo. DE21 16 D2
Frederick Av. DE24 21 E3
Frederick St. DE22 13 G2
Freehold St. DE22 13 G3
Freeman Av. DE23 19 G2
Freemantle Rd. DE3 12 C4
Freesia Clo. DE21 12 C6
French St. DE23 13 G5
Fresco Dri. DE23 18 C2
Friar Gate Ct. DE1 6 A3
Friar Gate Mews. DE1 6 A3
Friar Gate. DE1 6 A3
Friars Clo. DE22 9 F3
Friary Av. DE23 21 E3
Friary St. DE1 6 A3
Fritchley Clo. DE21 10 D5
Froggatt Clo. DE22 9 G1
Fulbrook Rd. DE24 18 D1
Fulham Rd. DE22 12 D3
Full St. DE1 6 B2
Fulmar Clo. DE24 21 E5

Furrows Clo. DE21 11 F3

Gable Ct. DE3 12 C6
Gainsborough Clo. DE21 11 E5
Gairloch Clo. DE24 19 G6
Galway Av. DE21 15 H4
Garden St. DE1 6 A1
Garfield Clo. DE23 19 F2
Garrick St. DE24 21 F2
Garry Clo. DE24 19 G6
Garsdale Walk. DE24 21 H2
Garth Cres. DE24 21 G3
Garthorpe Ct. DE21 10 D4
Gascoigne Dri. DE21 16 B3
Gaskell Av. DE23 19 H2
Gatcombe Clo. DE21 11 E4
Gayton Av. DE23 19 F2
Gayton Thorpe Clo.
DE23 18 D2
Gemma Clo. DE24 9 G2
George St. DE1 6 B3
George Yd. DE1 6 B3
Gerard Clo. DE21 16 D2
Gerard Ct. DE1 6 B4
Gerard St. DE1 6 B5
Gertrude Rd. DE21 10 D6
Gilbert Clo. DE21 16 C3
Gilbert St. DE24 21 G3
Gilderdale Way. DE21 11 F3
*Gillamore Ct, Keldolme La.
DE24 21 H2
Gisborne Clo. DE3 12 C4
Gisbourne Cres. DE22 9 F2
Gisbourne Grn. DE1 6 A1
Gladstone Clo. DE73 21 E5
Gladstone Dri. DE1 6 C3
Gladstone St. DE23 13 G6
Glaisdale Nook. DE24 21 H2
Glamis Clo. DE21 11 E4
Glastonbury Rd. DE24 21 H1
Gleadsmoss La. DE21 11 E5
Glebe Rise. DE23 13 F6
Glencroft Dri. DE24 19 G5
Glendale Dri. DE21 16 D2
Glendon Rd. DE24 19 G5
Gleneagles Clo. DE3 12 D5
Glenfield Cres. DE3 12 A5
Glengarry Way. DE24 19 C4
Glenmore Dri. DE24 19 G4
Glenmoy Clo. DE23 19 G1
Glenorchy Ct. DE21 11 E3
Glossop St. DE24 20 C1
Gloster St. DE24 15 E5
Goathland Rd. DE24 19 F6
Goldcrest Dri. DE21 16 D1
Golders Green Wk.
DE22 12 D2
*Goldstone Ct,
Gravel La. DE21 16 D3
Goodale St. DE23 14 B6
Goodrington Rd. DE21 11 F3
Goodsmoor Rd. DE23 19 G3
Goodwood Dri. DE24 21 H3
Gordon Rd. DE72 17 F6
Gordon Rd. DE23 14 B5
Gorse Clo. DE21 9 E2
Gorsty Leys. DE65 18 A6
Gosforth Rd. DE24 20 D1
Gower St. DE1 6 C4
Grafham Clo. DE73 21 F5
Grafton St. DE23 13 G5
Grampian Way. DE24 19 F5
Grandstand Rd. DE21 14 D1
Grange Av. DE3 19 H1
Grange Rd. DE24 21 G3
Grange St. DE23 14 C5
Grant Av. DE21 16 A2
Grantham Av. DE21 10 B4
Granville St. DE1 13 G3
Grasmere Av. DE21 16 C2
Grasmere Cres. DE24 19 H4
Grassthorpe Clo. DE21 11 E4
Grassy La. DE23 19 F2
Gravel La. DE21 16 D3
Gray Clo. DE23 19 G3
Grayling St. DE23 14 C5
Great Northern Rd. DE1 13 G3
Greatorex Av. DE24 20 D3
Green Acres. DE21 9 E1
Green Bank. DE21 16 B4
Green La. DE1 6 C5
Green La. DE21 21 G1
Green Park. DE22 12 D1
Greenburn Clo. DE23 19 F2
Greenfields Clo. DE21 15 E4
Greenfinch Clo. DE21 16 D1
Greenland Av. DE21 15 G5
Greenside Ct. DE3 12 A5

Greenway Clo. DE72 17
Greenway. DE65 18
Greenwich Dri Nth.
DE22 13
Greenwich Dri Sth.
DE22 12
Greenwood Av. DE21 10
Greenwood Ct. DE1 6
Gregory Walk. DE23 18
Grenfell Av. DE23 19
Gresham Rd. DE24 20
Grey St. DE1 6
Griffin Clo. DE24 2
Grimshaw Av. DE24 21
Grindlow Rd. DE21 10
Grosvenor St. DE24 20
Grovebury Dri. DE23 13
Gurney Av. DE24 21
Gypsy La. DE72 17

Haddon Clo. DE22 9
Haddon Dri. DE22 8
Haddon Dri. DE3 12
Haddon St. DE21 16
Haddon St. DE23 14
Haig St. DE24 1
Hailsham Clo. DE3 12
Hains Clo. DE24 20
Halifax Clo. DE21 16
Hall Dyke. DE21 1
Hall Park Clo. DE23 1
Hall St. DE24 2
Halstock Dri. DE24 2
Hambledon Dri. DE24 1
Hamblin Cres. DE24 1
Hamilton Clo. DE3 1
Hamilton Rd. DE23 14
Hamilton Rd. DE21 1
Hampden St. DE23 2
Hampshire Rd. DE21 1
Hampstead Dri. DE22 1
Hampton Clo. DE21 1
Hanbury Rd. DE21 1
Handel St. DE23 1
Handford St. DE22 1
Handyside St. DE1
Hanover Sq. DE22 1
Hansard Gate. DE21 1
Hanwell Way. DE22 1
Harcourt St. DE1
Hardhurst Rd. DE24 2
Hardwick Av. DE22
Hardwick St. DE24 2
Harebell Clo. DE21 1
Harepit Clo. DE24 2
Harewood Rd. DE22
Hargrave Av. DE72 1
Harlech Clo. DE21 1
Harlesden Av. DE22 1
Harlow Clo. DE24 2
Harold Ct. DE23
*Harpswell Clo,
Finningley Dri. DE22
Harpur Av. DE23
Harrier Way. DE24 1
Harriet St. DE23
Harringay Gdns. DE21 1
Harrington Av. DE72 1
Harrington Rd. DE23
Harrington St. DE23
Harrison St. DE22
Harrow St. DE24 1
Harrowgate Cres. DE21 1
Hartington Way. DE3
Hartland Dri. DE23
Hartshorne Rd. DE23
Harvest Way. DE21
Harvey Rd. DE24
Hasgill Clo. DE21
Haslams La. DE22
Haslemere Ct. DE23
Hassop Rd. DE21
Hastings St. DE23
Hatchmere Clo. DE21
Hatfield Rd. DE24
Hathern Clo. DE3
Hathersage Av. DE23
Havelock Rd. DE23
Haven Baulk Av. DE23
Haven Baulk La. DE23
*Haven Ct,
Keldolme La. DE24
Hawke St. DE22
Hawkshead Av. DE21
Hawthorn Av. DE24
Hawthorn Av. DE72

wthorn Cres. DE65 18 B6
wthorn St. DE24 20 C1
wtrey Gdns. DE24 21 F2
ydn Rd. DE21 10 D5
ydock Park Rd. DE24 21 E1
yes Av. DE72 19 G1
yfield Gdns. DE23 19 E2
ywood Clo. DE24 21 F4
zel Av. DE23 19 G2
zel Clo. DE65 18 B6
zel Dri. DE21 17 E2
zelwood Rd. DE21 10 D5
adingly Ct. DE23 19 F1
ath Av. DE23 13 F6
ath Ct. DE24 19 G5
ath La. DE65 18 B6
athcote Clo. DE24 21 G4
ather Clo. DE24 19 F6
ather Cres. DE23 19 F2
bden Clo. DE23 18 D3
brides Clo. DE24 19 G5
dgebank Ct. DE21 11 F3
dgerow Gdns. DE21 11 F3
dingham Way. DE3 18 B1
igham Clo. DE24 20 D5
lston Clo. DE24 21 G3
mlock Clo. DE21 10 D3
ndon Way. DE22 13 E2
nley Grn. DE22 12 D2
nry St. DE1 6 B1
reford Rd. DE21 10 B6
rmitage Av. DE72 17 F5
rmitage Ct. DE21 11 F4
ron Way. DE3 12 D5
ronswood Dri. DE21 16 C2
xham Walk. DE21 10 C4
yworth St. DE22 13 F2
ckling Clo. DE24 20 D5
gh St. DE1 14 D4
ghbury Clo. DE22 12 C2
ghfield La. DE21 15 F3
ghfield Mews. DE21 15 F3
ghfield Rd. DE23 19 F1
ghfield Rd. DE22 19 F2
ghfields Gdns. DE22 9 F6
ghgate Grn. DE22 13 E2
ghgrove Dri. DE73 21 E6
ilderstone Clo,
 Keldholme La. DE24 21 H2
l Brow. DE1 6 B5
l Clo. DE21 16 C3
l Cross Av. DE23 19 F2
l Cross Clo. DE23 19 E1
l Rise Clo. DE23 19 G1
l Top. DE21 10 C3
l View Gro. DE21 16 D2
lcrest Dri. DE73 21 F5
lcrest Rd. DE21 10 B6
lcroft Dri. DE72 17 F3
lside. DE65 18 A6
lside Av. DE21 15 G3
lside Cres. DE21 16 D3
lside Rd. DE21 16 D3
lsway. DE23 13 E6
lsway. DE73 21 F5
ton Clo. DE3 12 B6
ndscarth Cres. DE3 12 C6
bart Clo. DE3 12 C5
bkirk Dri. DE24 19 G6
dge Beck. DE24 19 H2
odthorpe Clo, Edwinstowe
 Rd. DE21 11 E4
lborn Dri. DE22 12 D1
lbrook Rd. DE24 21 F3
lcombe Clo. DE23 14 C6
lden Ct. DE24 21 F1
llies Rd. DE22 8 D2
llington Clo. DE21 10 C6
llis St. DE24 21 G4
llow Wood Av. DE23 19 F1
lloway Rd. DE24 21 F2
lly Ct. DE3 12 B6
llybrook Way. DE23 18 F2
lmere La. DE21 16 B5
lmes St. DE22 13 F4
lmfield. DE23 19 H1
olmoak Clo,
 Oakside Way. DE21 11 E3
lt Av. DE24 21 H3
ltlands Clo. DE24 21 E3
lyhead Dri. DE21 11 E3
lyrood Clo. DE1 6 D2
me Farm La. DE72 17 F2
me Farm Dri. DE22 9 F2
mesfield Dri. DE3 12 C5
pe Av. DE65 18 A5
pe St. DE73 6 D5
petoun St. DE23 20 B1

Hopton Clo. DE21 10 D5
Hornbeam Clo. DE21 10 C3
Horncastle Rd. DE21 10 B4
Hornsea Rd. DE21 10 B5
Horton St. DE23 14 D5
Horwood Av. DE23 13 G5
Hospital La. DE3 18 A1
*Houghton Ct,
 Morefern Dri. DE21 10 D4
Hounslow Rd. DE22 13 E2
Houston Clo. DE21 16 A2
Hoveton Clo. DE24 20 D5
Howard St. DE23 14 B5
Howden Clo. DE3 12 A5
Howe St. DE22 13 G2
Howth Clo. DE21 15 G3
Hoylake Ct. DE3 12 A5
Hoylake Dri. DE3 12 A4
Hubertshaw Clo. DE24 21 E4
Hucklow Ct. DE21 11 E3
Hulland St. DE1 14 D4
Hulland Vw. DE22 8 D5
Humber Clo. DE24 21 H3
Humbleton Dri. DE22 13 E2
Hunters Croft. DE24 14 B4
Huntingdon Grn. DE21 14 D2
Huntley Av. DE21 16 D1
Hutton St. DE24 20 D2
Hyde Park Rd. DE22 13 E1

INDUSTRIAL ESTATES:
*Beaufort Ct Ind Est,
 Mansfield Rd. DE21 9 H5
Castle Ward Ind Est.
 DE1 14 C3
Kingsway Ind Est.
 DE22 13 F3
Kingsway Retail Park.
 DE22 13 F3
Prime Enterprise Pk.
 DE1 6 D1
Prime Ind Est. DE23 14 D5
*Racecourse Ind Pk.,
 Mansfield Rd. DE21 9 H5
Raynesway Ind Est.
 DE24 15 G4
Robinson Ind Est.
 DE23 14 D5
The Parker Centre. DE1 9 H5
Industrial St. DE23 14 B5
Ingham Dri. DE3 12 B6
Ingle Clo. DE21 16 C3
Ingleby Av. DE23 19 H1
Inglewood Av. DE3 12 B4
Ingliston Clo. DE24 21 H3
Instow Dri. DE21 19 G3
Inveraray Clo. DE24 19 G5
Iona Clo. DE24 19 H5
Iron Gate. DE1 6 C3
Irving Pl. DE24 21 F2
Islay Rd. DE24 19 H4
Isleworth Dri. DE22 12 D2
Ismay Rd. DE21 15 G2
Ivernia Clo. DE23 19 G3
Ivy Ct. DE65 12 B6
Ivy Sq. DE23 14 D5
Ivybridge Clo. DE21 11 F3

Jacksdale Clo. DE22 8 D4
Jackson Av. DE3 12 D5
Jackson St. DE22 13 H3
James Clo. DE21 13 G2
Jarvis Ct. DE24 19 G6
Jarvis Rd. DE24 19 G6
Jasmine Clo. DE21 16 A3
Jedburgh Clo. DE24 19 G5
Jefferson Pl. DE24 21 E2
Jemison Clo. DE23 18 C2
Jessop Dri. DE24 21 E4
*John F. Kennedy Gdns,
 Ellendale Rd. DE21 16 A1
John Lombe Dri. DE1 6 C1
John St. DE1 14 C4
Johnson Av. DE24 21 E2
Joseph St. DE23 14 B6
Jubalton Clo. DE24 21 E3
Jubilee Rd. DE24 21 E4
Junction St. DE1 13 G3
Jury St. DE1 6 B3

Katrine Walk. DE24 19 G4
Kean Pl. DE24 21 F2
Keats Av. DE23 12 D6
Keble Clo. DE1 14 A3
Kedleston Clo. DE22 8 D4
Kedleston Gdns. DE1 6 A1

Kedleston Rd,
 Derby. DE22 6 A1
Kedleston Rd,
 Markeaton. DE22 8 C2
Kedleston St. DE1 6 A1
Kegworth Av. DE23 19 F2
Keldholme La. DE24 21 H2
Kelmoor Rd. DE24 21 G1
Kelso Walk. DE24 19 H6
Kemble Pl. DE24 21 F2
Kempton Park. DE24 20 D1
Kendal Walk. DE21 10 B4
Kenilworth Av. DE23 19 H2
Kensal Rise. DE24 20 A1
Kensington St. DE1 13 E1
Kensington St. DE1 6 A4
Kent St. DE1 15 E1
Kentish Ct. DE1 6 D1
Kernel Clo. DE23 13 E6
Kerry St. DE21 15 E1
Kershope Dri. DE21 11 E3
Kestrels Croft. DE24 19 G5
Keswick Av. DE23 19 H3
Kevin Clo. DE21 11 E6
Kew Gdns. DE22 13 E2
Keyhaven Clo. DE21 10 B5
Keynsham Clo. DE24 21 E1
Keys St. DE1 6 D2
Kibworth Clo. DE21 15 H3
Kildare St. DE21 15 H3
Killingworth Av. DE24 20 A5
Kilnsey Ct. DE23 18 D3
Kimberley Rd. DE72 17 F5
Kinder Walk. DE22 13 G3
King Alfred St. DE22 6 A5
King St. DE1 6 B1
Kingfisher Walk. DE24 19 H6
Kings Ct. DE1 6 B1
Kings Croft. DE22 9 F2
Kings Dri. DE23 13 E5
Kings Mead Clo. DE1 6 B1
Kings Mead Walk. DE1 6 A1
Kingsbury Rd. DE22 12 D2
Kingsclere Av. DE21 11 E4
Kingsland Clo. DE21 10 C3
Kingsley Rd. DE22 8 D2
Kingsley St. DE24 20 A3
Kingsmuir Rd. DE3 12 A4
Kingston St. DE1 9 F6
Kingsway. DE22 13 F2
Kingsway Ind Est. DE22 13 F3
Kingsway Retail Park.
 DE22 13 F3
Kingsway Pk Clo. DE22 13 F3
Kinross Av. DE21 10 B6
Kintyre Dri. DE24 19 G5
Kipling Clo. DE3 12 B6
Kirk Leys Av N. DE21 16 C4
Kirk Leys Av S. DE21 16 C4
Kirk St. DE1 9 G6
Kirkdale Av. DE21 16 D4
Kirkistown Clo. DE24 21 H3
Kirkland Way. DE24 19 H5
Kirkstead Clo. DE21 11 E5
Kitchener Av. DE23 19 G6
Knights Clo. DE24 19 G6
Knightsbridge. DE22 12 D2
Knoll Clo. DE23 18 D1
Knutsford Grn. DE21 16 A3
Kyle Gro. DE21 11 E3
Kynance Clo. DE24 21 H3

Laburnum Cres. DE22 13 D2
Laburnum Dri. DE22 13 E2
Ladbroke Gdns. DE22 12 D2
Ladybank Rd. DE3 12 A4
Ladybower Rd. DE21 16 D4
Ladycroft Paddock. DE22 9 E2
Ladygrove Cotts. DE22 9 E2
Ladysmith Rd. DE72 17 F5
Lake Dri. DE23 13 H1
Lakeside Dri. DE24 19 G5
*Lambe Ct,
 Morleston St. DE23 14 C4
Lambley Dri. DE22 8 C4
Lambourn Ct. DE22 9 F2
Lambourne Clo. DE22 9 F2
Lambrook Clo. DE3 12 A5
Lampeter Clo. DE24 11 E4
Lanark St. DE21 15 E1
Lancaster Walk. DE21 17 E2
Landemere. DE24 19 G5
Lang Rd. DE23 21 F3
Langdale Dri. DE21 16 B5
Langford Dri. DE3 12 B4
Langley Rd. DE21 11 E3
Langley St. DE22 13 G2
Langsett Dri. DE73 21 F6
Lanscombe Park Rd.
 DE22 9 E4

Lansdowne Av. DE24 21 E4
Lansing Gdns. DE21 16 A2
Lapwing Clo. DE24 19 G6
Larch Clo. DE22 8 D2
Larges St. DE1 13 H2
Lark Clo. DE21 19 F2
Larkhill Cres. DE24 20 A4
*Larkin Clo, Wordsworth
 Dri. DE24 20 A3
Larkspur Ct. DE21 11 E3
Lashley Gdns. DE21 10 C4
Lathbury Clo. DE21 10 B5
Lathkill Av. DE24 21 H2
Lathkill Rd. DE21 10 D5
Latimer Clo. DE23 13 E1
Latimer St. DE24 20 D2
Latrigg Clo. DE3 12 C6
Lauder Clo. DE24 19 H6
Launceston Rd. DE24 21 G3
Lavender Row. DE22 9 F4
*Laverstoke Ct,
 Peet St. DE22 13 H3
Lawn Av. DE22 8 D4
Lawn Heads Av. DE23 13 F5
Lawnside. DE21 16 D2
Lawnswood Clo. DE23 19 F1
Lawrence Av. DE72 11 E6
Lawrence St. DE23 20 A1
Lea Clo. DE21 9 E3
Lea Clo. DE23 15 F2
Lea Dri. DE3 12 B4
Leacroft Rd. DE23 14 C6
Leafenden Clo. DE22 9 F3
*Leafgreen La,
 Blagreaves La. DE23 19 F1
Leake St. DE1 13 G2
Leamington Clo. DE23 13 G6
Leander Clo. DE23 19 G1
Leaper St. DE1 13 H1
Leawood Gdns. DE21 11 E3
Ledbury Chase. DE24 19 G6
Ledbury Pl. DE21 14 D3
Leeds Pl. DE1 14 D3
Leeway. DE21 16 A3
Leicester St. DE22 13 G4
Leman St. DE22 13 G4
Lens Rd. DE22 8 C3
Lenten Av. DE21 15 F2
Leominster Dri. DE21 11 F3
Leonard St. DE22 13 G6
Leonard Walk. DE23 6 C6
Leopold St. DE1 14 A6
Leslie Clo. DE23 18 C1
Lewis Clo. DE23 14 A6
Lewiston Rd. DE21 16 A3
Lexington Rd. DE21 16 A2
Leybrook Clo. DE24 12 B4
Leyland Ct. DE1 9 E6
Leyland St. DE1 13 H1
Leylands. DE22 9 E5
Leytonstone Dri. DE22 12 D2
Lichfield Dri. DE24 21 F1
Lidgate Clo. DE3 12 A6
Lilac Av. DE24 21 F3
Lilac Clo. DE24 21 F3
Lilac Way. DE22 8 D4
Lilian Prime Clo. DE24 21 G1
Lilley St. DE24 21 G1
Lime Av. DE21 10 B4
Lime Av. DE23 12 B6
Lime Gro. DE21 15 H3
Lime La. DE21 11 E3
Lime Walk. DE23 13 G6
Limedale Av. DE21 16 A3
Limerick Rd. DE21 15 H3
Limes Av. DE3 12 B6
Limes Ct. DE3 12 B6
Limetree Clo. DE1 6 A3
Linacres Dri. DE73 21 F6
Lincoln Av. DE24 21 F1
Lindford Clo. DE21 10 D3
Lindisfarne Clo. DE21 19 G5
Lindon Dri. DE24 21 H2
Lindrick Clo. DE3 12 D6
Lindsey Clo. DE21 16 C2
Lingfield Rise. DE3 12 A4
Links Clo. DE24 20 D1
Linnet Clo. DE21 16 D1
Liskeard Dri. DE24 8 D2
*Lismore Ct, Tobermory
 Way. DE24 19 G4
Lister Clo. DE22 13 G4
Lister Ct. DE22 13 G4
Liston Dri. DE22 9 E6
Litchurch La. DE24 14 D5
Litchurch St. DE1 14 D6
Little Bridge St. DE1 6 A2
Little Eaton By-Pass.
 DE21 10 B1

Little Longstone Clo.
 DE3 12 C5
Little Noel St. DE22 13 G1
Littledale Clo. DE21 11 F3
Littleover Cres. DE23 13 G6
Littleover La. DE23 19 G1
Littlewoodbury Dri.
 DE23 18 D2
Litton Dri. DE21 16 D4
Liverpool St. DE21 10 C6
Liversage Pl. DE1 6 D5
Liversage Rd. DE1 6 D5
Liversage St. DE1 6 D5
Livingstone Rd. DE23 13 H6
Lloyd St. DE22 13 G2
Lochinvar Clo. DE21 16 D2
Lock Up Yd. DE1 6 C3
Lockington Clo. DE73 21 F6
Locko Ct. DE21 16 C2
Locko Rd. DE21 16 C2
Lockwood Rd. DE22 8 D2
Lodge La. DE1 6 A2
Lodge La. DE21 16 C3
Lodge Way. DE3 12 B5
Lombard St. DE22 12 C2
Lomond Av. DE24 19 H6
London Rd. DE24 21 F1
London Rd. DE1 6 D5
London Rd Diversion.
 DE1 14 C3
Longbridge La. DE24 20 D1
*Longdons Row,
 Church St. DE21 16 C3
Longford Clo. DE22 8 D4
Longford St. DE22 8 D6
Longlands La. DE65 18 B6
Longley La. DE21 16 B1
Longstock Clo. DE21 10 C4
Longstone Walk. DE1 6 B6
Longthorpe Clo. DE23 18 D2
Lonsdale Pl. DE22 13 G3
Lord St. DE24 20 D3
Lorne St. DE1 6 A6
Lorraine Clo. DE24 21 E5
Loscoe Rd. DE21 10 D5
Lothian Pl. DE21 14 D1
Lothlorien Clo. DE24 19 E2
Loudon St. DE23 14 C5
Lousie Greaves La.
 DE21 16 C2
Louvain Rd. DE23 13 F4
Lowe St. DE24 20 D2
Lower Dale Rd. DE23 14 A5
Lower Eley St. DE1 6 B6
Lower Green. DE65 18 B6
Lower Rd. DE22 8 A5
*Loxley Clo, Charingworth
 Rd. DE21 11 E4
Loxton Ct. DE3 12 B4
Loyne Clo. DE24 19 H6
Luccombe Dri. DE24 21 H4
Lucerne Rd. DE21 11 F3
Ludgate Walk. DE22 12 C2
Ludlow Clo. DE21 16 D3
Lulworth Clo. DE23 19 G2
Lundie Clo. DE24 19 G6
Lupin Clo. DE21 11 F3
Lychgate Clo. DE21 10 B3
Lydstep Clo. DE21 11 F3
Lyndhurst Gro. DE21 15 G3
Lyndhurst St. DE23 14 B5
Lynton St. DE22 13 H3
Lynwood Rd. DE24 20 A4
Lytham Clo. DE21 10 B4
Lyttleton St. DE22 13 F2

Macaulay St. DE24 20 A3
Mackenzie St. DE22 13 F2
Macklin St. DE1 6 B4
Mackworth Rd. DE1 13 G1
Macready Pl. DE24 21 F2
Madeley Ct. DE3 12 B6
Madeley St. DE23 14 C5
Madison Av. DE21 16 C6
Maidstone Dri. DE24 21 G3
Main Av. DE22 9 F1
Main Clo. DE24 21 G4
Main St. DE65 18 B6
Maine Dri. DE21 15 G1
Malcolm Gro. DE23 18 C1
Malcolm St. DE23 14 C5
Malham Rd. DE23 18 D2
Maltby Clo. DE24 9 E4
Malton Pl. DE21 10 B5
Malvern Clo. DE24 21 H4
Malvern Way. DE21 10 B5
Manchester St. DE22 13 G2
Manifold Dri. DE21 21 G1
Manor Av. DE23 13 F5

Manor Pk. DE72 17 E6
Manor Park Ct. DE22 13 E4
Manor Park Way. DE22 13 E4
Manor Rd. DE72 17 E6
Manor Rd. DE22 13 F4
Mansfield Rd. DE21 10 C3
Mansfield Rd. DE1 6 C2
Mansfield St. DE1 6 C1
Maple Av. DE23 19 G3
Maple Beck Ct. DE1 6 C1
Maple Dri. DE24 21 F3
Maple Dri. DE73 21 F6
Maple Gro. DE22 8 D1
Mapleton Rd. DE72 10 D5
Marchington Clo. DE22 9 E4
Maree Clo. DE24 19 H5
Marfleet Clo. DE3 12 B4
Margaret Av. DE21 15 F3
Margaret St. DE1 6 B1
Margreave Rd. DE21 10 C6
Marigold Clo. DE21 11 E3
Marina Dri,
  Allenton. DE24 21 E4
Marina Dri,
  Spondon. DE21 16 C2
Marjorie Rd. DE21 10 C5
Markeaton La. DE22 8 B6
Markeaton St. DE1 13 G1
Market Pl. DE1 6 C3
Markham Clo. DE11 6 C4
*Markham Ct,
  Chandlers Ford. DE21 10 C4
Marks Clo. DE23 19 G3
Marlborough Rd. DE24 20 C1
Marsden St. DE24 21 E2
Marsham Clo. DE3 12 C6
Marshgreen Clo. DE24 21 H4
Marston Clo. DE23 19 F3
Martin Dri. DE21 11 E5
Maryland Rd. DE21 16 A2
Marylebone Cres. DE22 12 D2
Masefield Av. DE23 19 G2
Masson Wk. DE22 13 H3
Matlock Rd. DE21 10 D4
Matthew St. DE24 21 E3
Matthews Way. DE23 18 C1
Max Rd. DE21 10 C6
Maxwell Av. DE22 8 D5
May St. DE22 6 A6
Mayfair Cres. DE22 12 C2
Mayfield Rd. DE21 10 C6
Maylands. DE72 17 F6
Maypole La. DE23 19 G1
*Mcgough Mews, Wordsworth
  Dri. DE24 20 A3
Mead Clo. DE24 20 A4
Meadow Clo. DE65 18 B5
Meadow Clo,
  Spondon. DE21 16 C3
Meadow La. DE24 15 G6
Meadow La,
  Cherrytree Hill. DE21 15 G3
Meadownook. DE24 21 H4
Meadow Rd. DE1 6 D3
Meadow View Clo. DE21 11 E5
Meadowgrass Clo. DE23 19 E2
Meadowlark Gro. DE21 10 D4
Mear Dri. DE72 17 F6
Meath Av. DE23 15 H4
Medina Clo. DE24 21 H3
Medway Dri. DE22 9 G1
Meerbrook Clo. DE21 11 E3
Megaloughton La. DE21 16 A4
Melandre Ct. DE22 13 G3
Melbourne Clo. DE24 8 D4
Melbourne Clo. DE1 12 C4
Melbourne St. DE1 6 C6
Melbrook Clo. DE3 12 B6
Melfort Clo. DE24 19 H6
Mellor St. DE24 20 D3
Melrose Clo. DE24 19 H6
Melton Av. DE23 19 F2
Memorial Rd. DE22 8 C3
Mendip Ct. DE21 10 C4
Menin Rd. DE22 8 C3
Mercaston Rd. DE21 10 D5
Merchant Av. DE21 16 A2
Merchant St. DE22 13 G2
Mercian Mews. DE1 16 B3
Merlin Grn. DE24 19 G4
Merridale Rd. DE23 19 F1
Merrill Way. DE24 20 D4
Merrybower Clo. DE24 19 F5
*Merthyr Ct, Leominster
  Dri. DE21 11 F3
Metcalfe Clo. DE24 21 G1
Meynell Ct. DE22 13 G3
Meynell St. DE23 14 A6
Michelle Clo. DE24 19 F5

Michigan Clo. DE21 16 A2
Micklecroft Gdns. DE23 18 C2
Mickleover By-Pass. DE3 12 C6
Mickleross Clo. DE3 12 B4
Middleton Av. DE23 13 F5
Middleton Dri. DE23 13 F5
Middleton St. DE23 14 B6
Midland Pl. DE1 14 D4
Midland Rd. DE1 14 D4
Midway. DE22 9 E4
Milburn Gdns. DE21 11 E3
Milbury Clo. DE21 10 D3
Mileash La. DE22 9 F4
Mileash Ter. DE22 9 F4
Milford St. DE1 6 B1
Mill Clo,
  Borrowash. DE72 17 F6
Mill Clo, Findern. DE65 18 B6
Mill Croft. DE3 12 B4
Mill Hill. DE24 21 H4
Mill Hill La. DE1 6 B6
Mill Hill Rd. DE23 14 B4
Mill La. DE3 12 B3
Mill Row. DE21 16 C2
Mill St. DE1 13 H2
Millbank Clo. DE22 12 C2
Milldale Rd. DE21 16 D4
Millers Ct. DE1 6 B1
Millom Clo. DE21 10 B4
Milton Clo. DE3 12 A4
Milton St. DE22 13 G3
Mimosa Cres. DE23 19 G3
Minster Rd. DE21 10 C3
Misterton Clo. DE22 9 E4
Mitcham Walk. DE22 12 D1
Moira Clo. DE21 11 E6
Molineaux St. DE23 14 C5
Monarch Dri. DE21 11 F3
Moncrieff Cres. DE21 11 E5
Mondello Dri. DE24 21 H3
Monk St. DE22 6 A4
Monks Clo. DE24 19 F5
Monmouth St. DE21 15 E1
Monsal Dri. DE21 16 D4
Montrose Clo. DE24 19 H4
Monyash Clo. DE21 10 D5
Moor Dri. DE24 21 G3
Moor End. DE21 16 D2
Moor La,
  Ockbrook. DE72 17 F1
Moor La,
  Osmaston. DE24 20 C3
Moor Rd. DE21 10 C2
Moor Way. DE21 10 C2
Moore St. DE23 14 B4
Moorgate. DE22 12 C2
Moorhead Av. DE21 21 E3
Moorland Rd. DE3 12 B5
Moorside Cres. DE24 20 A4
Moorway Croft. DE23 19 E2
Moorway La. DE23 19 E3
Moray Walk. DE21 10 B6
Morden Grn. DE22 12 D2
Morefern Dri. DE21 10 D4
Morledge. DE1 6 C3
Morleston St. DE23 14 C4
Morley Gdns. DE21 11 E5
Morley Rd. DE21 11 E6
Morley St. DE22 13 F2
Morlich Dri. DE24 19 G4
Morningside Clo. DE24 20 D4
Mornington Cres. DE22 13 E1
Morpeth Gdns. DE21 10 B4
Mortimer St. DE24 20 C1
Mosedale Clo. DE24 21 E1
Moss St. DE22 13 G4
Mostyn Av. DE23 19 F3
Mottistone Clo. DE24 21 H4
Moult Av. DE21 16 C3
Mount Carmel St. DE23 14 B4
Mount St. DE1 6 B6
*Mountbatten Clo,
  Walton Av. DE24 20 D4
Mountford Clo. DE21 11 E3
Mowbray Gdns. DE24 20 C1
Mowbray St. DE24 20 C1
Moy Av. DE24 19 H6
Muirfield Dri. DE3 12 D6
Mulberries Ct. DE22 9 ED2
Mull Clo. DE24 19 G5
Mullion Pl. DE24 21 G3
Mundy Clo. DE1 13 H2
Mundy St. DE1 13 H2
Munro Ct. DE24 19 G4
Murray Rd. DE3 12 C4
Murray St. DE24 21 F1
Muswell Rd. DE22 12 C2
Myers Clo. DE24 20 A5

Nairn Av. DE21 10 B6
Nairn Clo. DE24 19 G5
Namur Clo. DE22 13 F4
Napier Clo. DE3 12 B3
Napier St. DE22 13 F2
Naseby Clo. DE3 12 A4
Nearwood Dri. DE21 10 C3
Neilson St. DE24 21 E2
Nelson Clo. DE3 12 A4
Nelson St. DE1 14 D4
Nesfield Clo. DE24 21 H2
Ness Walk. DE22 9 E3
Netherwood Ct. DE22 8 C3
Nevinson Av. DE23 19 G2
Nevinson Dri. DE23 19 G2
Nevis Clo. DE24 19 G6
New Chester St. DE1 9 G6
New Mount Clo. DE23 19 G3
New Rd. DE22 9 F4
New St. DE1 14 D3
New St. DE22 17 F3
Orchard St. DE1 6 B2
New Zealand Sq. DE22 13 F2
Newark Rd. DE21 10 B4
Newbold Av. DE72 17 G6
Newbold Clo. DE73 21 F6
Newborough Rd. DE24 21 H3
Newbridge Cres. DE24 21 E4
Newdigate St. DE23 20 A1
Newel Walk. DE3 12 A6
Newhaven Rd. DE24 16 A2
Newland St. DE1 6 B4
Newlyn Dri. DE23 19 H1
Newmarket Ct. DE24 15 E6
Newmarket Dri. DE24 15 E6
Newport Ct. DE24 21 H3
Newquay Pl. DE24 21 H4
Newstead Av. DE21 15 F2
Newtons Walk. DE22 9 E6
Nicholas Clo. DE21 16 D2
Nicola Gdns. DE23 19 G4
Nidderdale Ct. DE24 21 H2
Nightingale Rd. DE24 20 C2
Noble St. DE1 14 D4
Noel St. DE22 13 G2
Norbury Clo. DE22 8 D4
*Norbury Ct,
  Norbury Clo. DE22 8 D4
Norbury Cres. DE23 19 F3
Norfolk St. DE23 14 C5
Norman Av. DE23 19 G1
Normanton La. DE23 13 F6
Normanton Rd. DE1 6 C5
North Av. DE22 9 F3
North Av. DE3 12 C4
North Clo. DE3 12 C5
North Par. DE1 6 B1
North Row. DE22 9 F4
North St. DE1 6 B1
North St. DE23 13 F5
North Walk. DE22 9 E6
Northacre Rd. DE21 11 E3
Northfield. DE24 19 F5
Northmead Dri. DE24 13 E4
Northumberland St.
  DE23 14 B5
Northwood Av. DE21 10 C6
Norwich St. DE21 10 B6
Norwood Clo. DE23 13 E3
Nottingham Rd. DE72 17 F6
Nottingham Rd. DE1 6 C2
Nottingham Rd. DE21 16 C4
Nuns St. DE1 13 H2
Nunsfield Dri. DE24 21 G2
Nursery Clo. DE72 17 F5
Nutwood Clo. DE22 9 F3

Oadby Rise. DE23 19 G3
Oak Clo, Allestree. DE22 8 D2
Oak Clo,
  Ockbrook. DE72 17 G2
Oak Cres. DE23 19 E1
Oak Dri. DE24 21 E2
Oak Dri. DE3 12 C5
Oak Ridge. DE21 10 B4
Oak St. DE23 14 B5
Oak Tree Ct. DE72 17 G6
Oakdale Gdns. DE21 11 E3
Oakham Clo. DE21 10 B4
Oaklands Av. DE23 19 E2
Oakleigh Av. DE23 15 F1
Oakover Dri. DE22 8 D3
Oakside Way. DE21 11 E3
Oaktree Av. DE24 20 B2
Oakwood Clo. DE23 19 E2
Oakwood Dri. DE21 11 E3
Offerton Av. DE23 19 H1
Old Blacksmiths Yd. DE1 6 B3
Old Chester Rd. DE1 6 B1
Old Church Clo. DE22 8 C1

Old Hall Av. DE24 21 G1
Old Hall Av. DE23 13 E6
Old Hall Rd. DE23 13 F6
Old La. DE22 9 F4
Old Mansfield Rd.
  DE21 10 A4
Old Vicarage Clo. DE23 13 F6
Oldbury Clo. DE21 10 D4
Olive Gro. DE21 15 G3
Olive St. DE22 13 H3
Oliver St. DE23 14 C6
Olton Rd. DE3 12 A4
Onslow Rd. DE3 12 B3
Opal Clo. DE21 10 D4
Orchard Clo. DE21 10 B2
Orchard Clo. DE23 19 F1
Orchard Clo. DE24 21 H4
Orchard Clo. DE72 17 F4
Orchard Ct. DE21 16 D2
Orchard La. DE21 10 B1
Orchard St. DE1 6 B2
Orchard St. DE3 12 B6
Orchard Way. DE73 21 F6
Ordish Av. DE21 15 F2
Oregon Way. DE21 16 A3
*Oriel Ct,
  Bloomfield Clo. DE1 14 C4
Orkney Clo. DE24 19 G5
Ormskirk Rise. DE21 16 D3
Osborne St. DE1 14 D4
Osmaston Pk Rd. DE24 20 A1
Osmaston Rd. DE1 6 C5
Osmaston Rd. DE24 20 C1
Osnabruck Sq. DE1 6 C3
Osprey Clo. DE24 19 H6
Osterley Grn. DE22 13 E3
Oswestry Clo. DE21 11 F3
Otter St. DE1 9 F6
Otterburn Dri. DE22 8 C4
Oulton Clo. DE24 20 D4
Outram Way. DE24 19 G6
Oval Ct. DE23 19 F1
Overdale Rd. DE23 13 H5
Owlers La. DE23 13 E5
Owlswick Clo. DE23 18 D1
Oxenhope Clo. DE23 18 C2
Oxford St. DE1 14 D4
Oxford St. DE21 16 C3
Oxton Way. DE24 19 H6
*Oxwich Ct,
  Leominster Dri. DE21 11 F3

*Paddock Croft, Chandlers
  Ford. DE21 10 C4
Padley Clo. DE21 9 G1
Padstow Clo. DE24 19 F5
Padstow Rd. DE24 21 H3
Palatine Gro. DE23 18 D1
Pall Mall. DE21 10 C2
Palm Clo. DE23 13 E6
Palmerston St. DE23 13 G5
Parcel Ter. DE22 13 G3
Pares Way. DE72 17 G2
Park Dri. DE23 13 F6
Park Gro. DE22 9 E6
Park Hill Dri. DE23 19 H1
Park La, Allestree. DE22 9 F2
Park La,
  Littleover. DE23 13 F6
Park Leys Ct. DE21 16 B3
Park Rd,
  Mickleover. DE3 12 B5
Park Rd,
  Spondon. DE21 16 B3
Park St. DE1 14 D4
Park View Clo. DE22 9 E2
Parker Clo. DE1 6 A1
Parker St. DE1 6 A1
Parkfields Dri. DE22 9 E6
Parkside Rd. DE21 15 G2
Parkstone Ct. DE23 12 A5
Parliament Clo. DE22 13 G4
Parliament St. DE22 13 G4
Partridge Way. DE3 13 E5
Pastures Av. DE23 18 D1
Pastures Hill. DE23 13 E6
Paterson Av. DE21 15 H2
Patmore Sq. DE23 19 H2
*Patten Ct, Wordsworth Dri.
  DE24 20 A3
Pavilion Rd. DE23 19 F1
Paxton Clo. DE3 12 B5
Payne St. DE22 13 G1
Peach St. DE22 13 G1
Peacock Gro. DE22 19 E2
Peak Dri. DE24 20 A1
Pear Tree Cres. DE32 20 B1
Pear Tree Rd. DE23 14 B5

Pear Tree St. DE23 14
Pearl Clo. DE21 10
Peartree Ct. DE21 10
Peckham Gdns. DE22 13
Peebles Clo. DE24 19
Peel St. DE22 13
Peers Clo. DE21 11
Peet St. DE22 13
Peggs Walk. DE23 19
Pegwell Clo. DE23 19
Pelham St. DE22 6
Pembroke St. DE21 10
Penallton Clo. DE24 21
Pendennis Clo. DE24 21
Pendlebury Dri. DE3 12
Pendleside Way. DE23 18
Penge Rd. DE22 12
Penny Long La. DE22 9
Pennycress Clo. DE23 18
Penrhyn Av. DE23 13
Penrith Pl. DE21 10
Pentewen Clo. DE22 9
*Pentland Clo,
  Bonnyrigg Dri. DE21 10
Penzance Rd. DE24 21
Percy St. DE22 13
Peregrine Ct. DE24 19
Perth Clo. DE3 12
Perth St. DE21 10
Peterborough St. DE21 10
Peterhouse Ter. DE23 11
Peterlee Pl. DE24 21
Petersham Dri. DE24 11
Peveril Av. DE72 17
Peveril St. DE24 20
Pheasant Fld Dri. DE21 17
Phoenix St. DE1 6
Pickering Rise. DE21 10
Pilgrims Way. DE24 19
Pillar Ct. DE3 12
Pimlico. DE22 13
Pinecroft Ct. DE21 11
Pintail Dri. DE24 19
Pittar St. DE22 6
Plantain Gdns. DE23 19
*Plimsoll Ct,
  Warner St. DE22 13
Plimsoll St. DE22 13
Plough Gate. DE22 9
Ploughfield Clo. DE23 19
Pollards Oaks. DE72 17
Ponsonby Ter. DE1 6
Pontefract St. DE24 20
Pontypool Clo. DE21 11
Poole St. DE24 20
Poplar Av. DE21 16
Poplar Clo. DE24 21
Poplar Nook. DE22 9
Poplar Rd. DE72 9
*Porlock Clo, Countisbury
  Dri. DE21 10
Porter Rd. DE23 14
Porters La,
  Breadsall. DE21 10
Porters La,
  Findern. DE65 18
Porters Rd. DE23 13
Portland Clo. DE3 12
Portland St. DE23 14
Portman Chase. DE24 19
Portreath Dri. DE22 9
Potter St. DE21 16
Powell St. DE23 19
Poyser Av. DE21 10
Prescot Clo. DE3 12
Prestbury Clo. DE24 11
Pride Pk. DE24 15
Priestland Av. DE21 11
Prime Enterprise Pk. DE1 6
Prime Ind Est. DE23 14
Prime Park Way. DE1 6
Primrose Clo. DE3 12
Primula Way. DE23 19
Prince Charles Av. DE22 12
Princes Clo. DE23 14
Princes St. DE23 13
Princess Clo. DE72 17
Priors Barn Clo. DE72 17
Priorway Av. DE72 17
Pritchett Dri. DE23 18
Provident St. DE23 13
Pulborough Gdns. DE23 18
Pullman Rd. DE23 15
Putney Clo. DE23 13
Pybus St. DE22 13
*Pykestone Clo,
  Silverburn Dri. DE24 19

Quantock Clo. DE24 19

32

n Dri. DE22 8 C3
rn St. DE1 6 A1
rn Way. DE1 6 A1
ndon Heights. DE22 8 D3
ndon View. DE22 8 D3
en Mary Ct. DE22 9 F6
en St. DE1 6 B2
ens Dri. DE23 13 F5
ensferry Gdns. DE24 20 D4
ensland Clo. DE3 12 C3
ensway. DE22 13 F1
khill Rd. DE24 19 F6
ings Way. DE72 17 G6
rn Rise. DE23 19 G3
wn Av. DE23 19 F1
ecourse Ind Pk,
  lansfield Rd. DE1 9 H5
ourne La. DE22 12 B2
ourne St. DE22 13 F2
liffe Av. DE21 15 F1
liffe Dri. DE22 13 G4
st Dri. DE24 21 C1
or St. DE21 10 B6
tock Gdns. DE21 10 C4
tone Clo. DE21 11 E3
an Av. DE22 13 F2
vay Ter. DE1 14 D3
ham Gdns. DE24 21 F3
er Dri. DE21 15 G1
gh St. DE22 13 F2
blers Dri. DE21 11 F3
sdean Clo. DE21 10 B5
shaw Way. DE22 13 G4
olph Rd. DE23 20 A1
lagh Gdns. DE21 13 E1
moor Clo. DE3 12 C4
och Clo. DE21 9 E3
och Clo. DE24 16 D3
vorth Clo. DE24 20 D5
che Ct,
  orleston St. DE23 14 C4
n St. DE22 13 H4
nscourt Rd. DE22 13 F1
nscroft Dri. DE21 15 G2
nsdale Rd. DE22 8 C2
ton St. DE23 14 A5
inson Av. DE23 20 A2
esway. DE24 15 G5
24 15 G4
esway Pk Dri. DE24 15 H6
esway. DE21 15 G3
er St. DE21 16 C2
ory La. DE21 10 B2
lver Clo. DE23 19 G2
ury Clo. DE1 13 G3
ar Gdns. DE21 10 B5
and Clo. DE24 20 A4
ires Rd. DE73 21 F6
uth Clo. DE24 21 H4
haw St. DE1 13 H1
tart Clo. DE21 16 D1
ring Croft. DE23 19 G2
vood Rd. DE24 19 H5
es Rd. DE23 14 C6
ncy Clo. DE23 19 F1
nt St. DE1 14 C1
ald Rd N. DE21 15 G1
ald Rd S. DE21 15 F2
ald St. DE21 14 C5
Clo. DE21 11 E4
te Dri. DE22 12 D1
s St. DE23 6 B6
ew St. DE1 10 C6
on Av. DE23 13 G6
rd Clo. DE21 10 B4
rdson St. DE22 13 G2
mond Av. DE23 19 F1
mond Rd. DE21 15 G2
mond Rd. DE23 14 C6
ngs Way. DE22 6 A6
way Av. DE23 19 F1
wood Clo. DE21 19 F1
y Ct. DE3 12 A4
dale Clo. DE21 19 G5
vood Clo. DE21 10 C5
Cres. DE21 10 C5
hall Clo. DE23 19 F1
St. DE1 6 C1
Croft Rd. DE22 9 E2
Rd. DE1 6 D2
ia Clo. DE21 11 F3
s Cross. DE72 17 F6
son Ind Est. DE23 14 D5
ster Clo. DE24 21 F2
ester Clo. DE24 21 F3
ey Clo. DE21 10 C3

*Rockbourne Clo, Kendolme La. DE22 21 H2
Rockhouse Rd. DE24 21 F3
Rockingham Clo. DE22 9 G2
Rodney Walk. DE23 18 C1
Rodsley Cres. DE23 19 F3
Roe Farm La. DE21 15 E1
Roe Walk. DE23 14 B5
Roehampton Dri. DE22 12 D1
Roman Rd. DE1 9 G6
Romsley Clo. DE3 12 B4
Rona Clo. DE24 19 H4
Ronald Clo. DE23 18 C1
Royal Gro. DE21 11 F3
Roosevelt Av. DE21 16 A1
Rosamonds Ride. DE23 19 G1
Rose Av. DE72 17 G6
Rose Hill St. DE23 14 C5
*Roseberry Ct,
  Appledore Dri. DE21 11 E4
Rosedale Av. DE24 21 F2
Rosemary Dri. DE24 21 F4
Rosemoor La. DE21 11 E4
Rosemount Ct. DE22 8 C3
Rosengrave St. DE1 6 B5
Rosenheath Clo. DE21 19 H3
*Rosette Clo,
  Dahlia Dri. DE21 11 F3
Rosewood Clo. DE24 21 G1
Ross Walk. DE21 10 B4
Rossington Dri. DE23 18 C2
Rosslyn Gdns. DE24 21 F3
Rothbury Pl. DE21 10 C4
Rothesay Clo. DE24 19 G4
Rothwell Rd. DE3 12 B4
Rough Heanor Rd. DE3 12 D5
Roughton Clo. DE3 18 B1
Rowan Clo. DE21 16 A3
Rowan Clo. DE24 19 F5
Rowan Park Clo. DE23 19 G2
Rowditch Av. DE22 13 G3
Rowditch Pl. DE22 13 G3
Rowena Clo. DE24 21 E2
Rowland St. DE24 20 D3
Rowley Gdns. DE23 19 F1
Rowley La. DE23 19 F2
Rowsley Av. DE23 13 G6
Roxburgh Av. DE21 10 C6
Royal Clo. DE72 17 F6
Royal Hill Rd. DE21 16 B2
Roydon Clo. DE3 12 A4
Rudyard Av. DE21 16 C2
Rugby St. DE22 15 F6
Ruislip Clo. DE22 9 G1
Rupert Rd. DE21 10 D6
Rushcliffe Gdns. DE21 15 F2
Rushcliffe Av. DE21 15 F2
Rushdale Av. DE23 19 G2
Ruskin Rd. DE1 9 F6
Ruskin Way. DE21 19 E1
Russell St. DE23 14 D6
Russet Clo. DE65 11 E4
*Rutherford Rise,
  Morefern Dri. DE21 10 D4
Rutland Av. DE72 17 G5
Rutland Dri. DE3 14 B6
Rutland St. DE23 14 B6
Ryal Clo. DE72 17 G2
Ryan Clo. DE24 19 G5
Rydal Clo. DE21 9 E2
Rye Clo. DE21 10 C3
Ryedale Gdns. DE21 19 F4
Ryegrass Rd. DE21 11 F3
Rykneld Clo. DE23 18 C2
Rykneld Rd. DE23 18 B3
Rykneld Way. DE23 18 B3
Rymill Dri. DE21 10 C4
Sacheverel St. DE1 6 C5
Sackville St. DE1 20 A1
Saddleworth Wk. DE24 20 D5
Sadler Gate. DE1 6 B3
Saffron Dri. DE1 10 D4
St Agnes Av. DE22 9 E2
St Albans Rd. DE22 13 F4
St Alkmunds Way. DE1 6 B2
St Andrews Vw. DE21 10 C5
St Annes Ct. DE1 13 H1
St Augustine St. DE23 14 A6
St Brides Walk. DE21 13 E1
St Chads Rd. DE23 14 A5
St Clares Clo. DE23 13 G5
St Cuthberts Rd. DE22 13 H2
St Davids Clo. DE21 13 F4
St Edmunds Clo. DE22 9 F2
St Giles Rd. DE23 14 B6
St Helens St. DE1 6 B2
St Hughs Clo. DE22 9 F4

St James Rd. DE23 14 B6
St James's St. DE1 6 C3
St Johns Av. DE21 15 H3
St Johns Clo. DE22 8 D3
St Johns Rd. DE21 15 H3
St Johns Ter. DE1 6 A2
St Marks Rd. DE21 14 D1
St Marys Bri. DE1 6 C2
St Marys Clo. DE24 21 F3
St Marys Ct. DE1 6 C1
St Marys Gate. DE1 6 B3
St Marys Mews. DE1 6 B1
St Marys Wharf Rd. DE1 6 D1
St Matthews Walk. DE22 9 F4
St Maws Clo. DE22 8 D2
St Mellion Clo. DE3 12 D6
St Michaels Clo. DE65 21 H2
St Michaels La. DE1 6 C2
*St Michaels View,
  Branksome Av. DE24 21 H2
St Nicholas Clo. DE22 8 D3
St Pancras Way. DE1 6 D1
St Pauls Rd. DE1 9 G6
St Peters Church Yd. DE1 6 C4
St Peters St. DE1 6 C4
St Peters Way. DE1 6 C4
St Quenten Clo. DE22 13 F5
St Stephens Clo. DE72 17 F6
St Stephens Clo. DE23 19 G2
St Swithuns Clo. DE22 13 F4
St Thomas Rd. DE23 14 B6
St Werburghs Churchyard.
  DE1 6 B3
St Werburghs Vw. DE21 16 B3
St Wystans Rd. DE22 13 F4
Sale St. DE23 14 C5
Salisbury St. DE23 14 B4
Sallywood Clo. DE24 19 G6
Saltburn Clo. ED21 10 B4
Sancroft Rd. DE21 16 C2
Sandalwood Clo. DE21 21 H2
*Sandbach Clo,
  Gleadmoss La. DE21 11 E5
Sanderson Rd. DE21 16 A2
Sandfield Clo. DE21 11 E5
Sandgate Clo. DE24 21 G3
Sandown Av. DE3 12 A4
Sandown Rd. DE24 20 D1
Sandringham Dri. DE21 16 D3
Sandringham Rd. DE21 10 C4
Santolina Clo. DE21 10 D4
Sapperton Clo. DE23 19 F3
Saundersfoot Way. DE21 11 F3
Saxondale Av. DE3 12 B4
Scarborough Rise. DE21 10 A5
Scarcliffe Clo. DE24 20 D5
Scarsdale Av. DE3 13 F5
Scarsdale Av. DE22 8 D3
School La. DE73 21 F6
Scott St. DE23 14 B6
Scropton Walk..DE24 21 E5
Seagrave Clo. DE21 11 E5
Seale St. DE1 6 C1
Searl St. DE1 6 A2
Seascale Clo. DE21 10 B4
Seaton Clo. DE3 12 A5
Sedgebrook Clo. DE21 10 C4
Sedgefield Grn. DE3 12 A6
Sefton Rd. DE21 15 F1
Selbourne St. DE24 15 E5
Selkirk St. DE21 10 B6
Selworthy Clo. DE21 10 D4
Selwyn St. DE1 13 F2
Serina Av. DE23 19 G1
Sevenlands Dri. DE24 21 H4
Sevenoaks Av. DE22 12 C2
Severn St. DE24 21 E1
Severn Vale Clo. DE22 9 G1
Seymour St. DE22 13 F2
Shacklecross Clo. DE72 17 F6
Shaftesbury Cres. DE23 14 C6
Shaftesbury St Sth.
  DE23 14 C6
Shaftesbury St. DE23 14 D5
Shakespeare St. DE24 15 E5
Shaldon Dri. DE23 13 G6
Shalfleet Dri. DE24 21 H3
Shamrock St. DE23 13 G6
*Shandwick Ct,
  Cairngorm Dri. DE24 19 G5
Shannon Clo. DE23 19 G2
Shannon Sq. DE21 15 H3
Shardlow Rd. DE24 21 F1
Shaw Grn. DE21 13 G2
Shaw St. DE22 13 G2
Shearwater Clo. DE21 13 G2
Sheffield Pl. DE1 14 C1
Sheldon Clo. DE23 21 E5
Shelley Dri. DE24 20 A3

Shelmory Clo. DE24 20 D3
Shelton Dri. DE24 21 E5
Shelton Ter. DE22 13 G3
Shenington Way. DE21 11 E4
Shepherd St. DE23 13 F6
Sheridan St. DE24 20 A4
Sherston Clo. DE21 11 E3
Sherwin St. DE22 8 D6
Sherwood Av. DE72 17 G5
Sherwood Av. DE21 15 G1
Sherwood Av. DE24 19 G4
Sherwood St. DE22 13 H4
Shetland Clo. DE21 10 B6
Shipley Walk. DE24 20 D5
Shire Oaks Clo. DE23 19 F2
*Shirland Ct,
  Smisby Way. DE24 21 E5
Shirley Rd. DE21 10 C5
Shorewell Gdns. DE21 21 H3
Short Av. DE22 9 F1
Shottle Walk. DE24 20 D5
*Shrewsbury Clo,
  Leominster Dri. DE21 11 F3
Shropshire Av. DE21 15 F1
Siddals Rd. DE1 6 D4
Siddals La. DE22 9 F2
Siddons St. DE24 21 F2
Sidmouth Clo. DE24 21 H2
Sidney St. DE1 14 C4
Silver Hill Rd. DE23 14 B5
Silver Hill Rd. DE21 16 D4
Silverburn Dri. DE21 10 D4
Silverton Av. DE24 19 F6
Silvey Gro. DE21 16 D3
Simcoe Leys. DE73 21 F6
Simpson St. DE24 21 E2
Sims Av. DE1 13 G2
Sinclair Clo. DE24 19 G5
Sinfin Av. DE24 20 D4
Sinfin Fields Cres. DE24 20 D4
Sinfin La. DE24 20 A4
Sir Frank Whittle Rd.
  DE21 9 H6
Siskin Dri. DE24 19 G5
Sitwell Clo. DE24 16 C3
Sitwell St. DE1 6 C5
Sitwell St. DE21 16 C3
Skiddaw Dri. DE3 12 C6
Skipton Grn. DE21 10 A5
Skylark Way. DE24 19 G4
Slack La. DE22 13 F2
Slaidburn Clo. DE3 12 C6
Slaney Clo. DE24 21 E2
Slater Av. DE1 13 G2
Sledmere Clo. DE24 21 H2
*Slindon Croft, Derrington
  Leys. DE24 21 H2
Sloane Rd. DE22 12 D2
Smalley Dri. DE21 11 E3
Smisby Way. DE24 21 E5
Snelford Clo. DE3 12 A4
Snelsmoor La. DE73 21 G6
Snelston Cres. DE23 13 F5
Society Pl. DE23 14 B5
*Solway Clo, Caldermill
  Dri. DE21 10 D4
Somerby Way. DE21 10 C4
Somersal Clo. DE24 20 D5
Somerset St. DE21 10 B6
Somme Rd. DE22 8 C3
South Av. DE22 9 F3
South Av. DE23 13 F6
South Av. DE73 21 E5
South Brae Clo. DE23 19 F2
South Ct. DE3 12 B6
South Dri. DE21 15 G2
South Dri. DE3 9 F6
South Dri. DE3 12 D5
South St. DE21 21 F5
South St. DE1 13 H2
Southcroft. DE23 19 G4
Southdown Clo. DE23 19 F6
Southgate Clo. DE3 12 A4
Southmead Way. DE22 13 E4
Southwark Clo. DE3 13 E2
Southwood St. DE24 21 E1
Sovereign Way. DE21 11 G3
Sowter Rd. DE1 6 C2
Sowter Sq. DE1 6 B3
Spa Cft. DE1 10 B6
Spa La. DE21 10 B6
Sparrow Clo. DE24 19 G4
Sparrowdale Rd. DE24 19 G4
Speedwell Clo. DE21 11 F3
Spenback Dri. DE22 9 G1
Spencer Av. DE24 20 D4
Spencer Av. DE23 21 F1
Spindletree Dri. DE21 10 C4

Spinney Clo. DE22 9 F4
Spinney Rd. DE21 13 H5
Spinney Rd. DE21 10 D6
Spoonleywood Ct. DE23 18 D2
Spring Gdns. DE21 10 D6
Spring St. DE22 6 A5
Springdale Ct. DE24 12 C6
Springfield Clo. DE3 13 E5
Springfield Rd. DE24 16 A2
Springfield Rd. DE73 21 E6
Springwood Dri. DE21 11 E4
Squires Way. DE3 18 D2
Stables St. DE22 13 G2
Stafford St. DE1 6 A3
Staines Clo. DE3 12 A5
Staithes Walk. DE21 10 A4
Staker La. DE3 18 B2
Staker Way. DE3 18 B2
Stamford St. DE24 21 F5
Stangate Grn. DE3 12 C5
Stanhope Rd. DE3 12 C4
Stanhope St. DE23 14 B5
Stanier Way. DE21 15 G4
Stanley Clo. DE22 9 F5
Stanley Rd. DE24 21 E2
Stanley Rd. DE23 15 G3
Stanley St. DE22 13 G2
Stanstead Rd. DE3 12 A4
Stanton St. DE23 14 A5
Starcross Ct. DE3 12 A4
Statham St. DE22 9 E6
Station Rd. DE72 17 E6
Station Rd. DE21 10 B2
Station Rd. DE3 12 B5
Station Rd. DE21 16 B4
Staunton Av. DE23 19 G3
Staveley Clo. DE24 21 E5
Staverton Dri. DE3 12 B4
Steeple Clo. DE21 10 C4
Stenson Av. DE23 19 G2
Stenson Rd. DE23 14 A6
Stenson Rd. DE24 19 E6
Stephensons Way.
  DE21 15 G4
Stepping Clo. DE1 13 G2
Stepping La. DE1 13 G2
Stevenage Clo. DE24 21 F4
Stevenson Pl. DE23 19 E1
Stewart Clo. DE21 16 D2
Stiles Rd. DE21 21 G1
Stirling Clo. DE24 10 B5
Stockbrook Rd. DE22 13 G4
Stockbrook St. DE22 6 A5
Stocker Av. DE24 21 H2
Stone Clo. DE21 16 C2
Stone Dri. DE21 16 A3
Stonebroom Wk. DE24 21 E5
Stonechat Clo. DE3 13 E5
Stonehill Rd. DE23 14 A5
Stonesby Clo. DE21 10 D4
Stonesdale Ct. DE24 21 H2
Stoney Cross. DE21 16 C4
Stoney Flats Cres. DE21 11 E6
Stoney La. DE21 16 C4
Stoneyhurst Ct. DE24 21 E5
Stoodley Pike Gdns.
  DE22 8 C4
Stores Rd. DE1 10 A6
Stornoway Clo. DE24 19 G5
Stourport Dri. DE3 21 F5
Stowmarket Dri. DE21 10 D5
Strand. DE1 6 B3
Stratford Rd. DE21 10 B4
Strathaven Ct. DE21 16 C3
Strathmore Av. DE21 21 F3
Streatham Rd. DE22 13 E5
Stretton Clo. DE3 12 B6
Stroma Clo. DE21 19 H4
Strutt St. DE23 14 C5
Stuart St. DE1 6 C2
Sudbury Clo. DE1 13 H3
Sudbury St. DE1 13 H3
Suffolk Av. DE21 15 F1
Summerbrook Ct. DE22 6 A5
Summerwood Ct. DE23 19 G2
Sun St. DE22 6 A5
Sunart Clo. DE24 19 H6
Sundew Clo. DE21 16 D3
Sundown Av. DE23 19 G2
Sunningdale Av. DE21 16 C2
Sunny Grove. DE21 16 C3
Sunnydale Av. DE23 19 G2
Sunnyhill Av. DE23 19 F4
Surbiton Clo. DE3 13 E2
Surrey St. DE22 13 G2
Sussex Circus. DE21 10 B6
Sutherland Rd. DE23 14 C6
Sutton Av. DE73 21 E5
Sutton Clo. DE22 13 F1

Sutton Dri. DE24 21 E4
Sutton Ho. DE24 21 H4
Swaledale Ct. DE24 21 H2
*Swallow Clo,
 Partridge Way. DE3 13 E5
Swanmore Rd. DE23 19 E1
Swanwick Gdns. DE21 10 D4
Swarkestone Dri. DE23 19 F3
Swayfield Clo. DE3 12 A5
Sweet Briar Clo. DE24 21 F4
Swift Clo. DE3 13 E4
Swinburne St. DE1 6 B6
Swinderby Dri. DE21 11 E4
Sycamore Av. DE22 8 D2
Sycamore Av. DE65 18 B6
Sycamore Ct. DE21 16 C3
Sydenham Rd. DE22 12 D1
Sydney Clo. DE3 12 C4

Taddington Clo. DE21 10 C5
Taddington Rd. DE21 10 C5
Talbot St. DE1 6 A4
*Talgarth Clo,
 Leominster Dri. DE21 11 F3
Tamar Av. DE22 8 D2
Tansley Rise. DE21 10 D4
Taplow Clo. DE3 12 A5
Tasman Clo. DE3 12 C4
Taunton Clo. DE24 21 H1
Taverners Cres. DE23 19 F1
Tavistock Clo. DE21 19 F5
Tawny Way. DE23 18 D2
Tay Clo. DE24 19 G6
Tay Walk. DE22 9 E3
Taylor St. DE24 15 E5
Tayside Clo. DE24 19 F5
Tedworth Av. DE24 19 F6
Telford Clo. DE3 19 F6
Templar Clo. DE24 19 F6
Temple St. DE23 14 B5
Tenant St. DE1 6 C3
Tennessee Rd. DE21 15 G1
Tennyson St. DE24 20 D1
Terry Pl. DE24 21 E2
*Teviot Pl, Bonnyrigg
 Dri. ED21 10 D4
Tewkesbury Cres. DE21 10 B5
Thackeray St. DE24 20 A3
Thames Clo. DE22 12 C2
Thanet Dri. DE24 21 F3
The Avenue. DE21 15 G2
The Avenue. DE1 6 C5
The Chase. DE24 20 A4
The Circle. DE24 19 H4
The Close. DE22 9 F3
The Close. DE23 13 G5
The Cock Pitt. DE1 6 D4
The Court. DE24 21 G2
The Covert. DE21 16 C3
The Crescent. DE24 21 E3
The Crescent. DE21 15 F2
The Crest. DE22 9 E4
The Croft. DE23 19 G1
The Eyrie. DE23 19 G5
The Green. DE65 18 B6
The Green. DE22 8 D4
The Green. DE3 12 B6
The Grove. DE3 12 B5
The Hayes. DE65 18 A6
The Hill. DE22 9 F4
The Hollow. DE23 19 F1
The Hollow. DE23 18 B1
The Hollows. DE3 12 B6
The Orchards. DE22 8 D3
The Paddocks. DE72 17 F3
The Parade. DE3 12 B6
The Parker Centre. DE1 9 H5
The Pingle. DE22 9 E2
The Pingle. DE21 16 D3
The Poplars. DE22 9 F2
The Riddings. DE22 9 E2
The Ridings. DE72 17 G2
The Rise. DE22 9 E4
The Settlement. DE22 17 F3
The Sidings. DE21 15 G4
The Spinney. DE72 17 G6
The Spot. DE1 6 C4
The Square. DE3 12 B6
The Underpass. DE1 6 D2
The Walk. DE23 19 G3
Theatre Walk. DE1 6 D4
Thirlmere Av. DE22 9 E2
Thirsk Pl. DE24 20 D2
Thistledown Clo. DE22 9 F3
*Thoresby Clo,
 Edinstowe Rd. DE21 11 E4
Thorn Clo. DE22 9 E2
Thorn St. DE23 14 B5
Thorndike Av. DE24 21 F1

Thorness Clo. DE24 21 H4
Thornhill Rd. DE22 13 F3
Thornhill Rd. DE23 13 F6
Thorntree La. DE1 6 C4
Thorpe Dri. DE3 12 B4
Thorpelands Dri. DE22 8 D5
Thrushton Clo. DE65 18 A6
Thruxton Clo. DE24 21 H3
Thurcroft Clo. DE22 13 F2
Thurlow Ct. DE21 10 D5
Thyme Clo. DE23 19 F4
Tiber Dri. DE24 21 H3
Tickham Av. DE24 19 F6
Ticknall Walk. DE23 19 G3
Tideswell Rd. DE21 10 C5
Tilbury Pl. DE24 21 F3
Tiller Clo. DE23 19 E2
Timbersbrook Clo. DE21 11 E4
Timsbury Ct. DE21 10 C4
Tintagel Clo. DE23 14 C5
Tiree Clo. ED24 19 H4
*Tissington Dri,
 Smalley Dri. DE21 11 E3
Tiverton Clo. DE3 12 B4
Tivoli Gdns. DE1 13 H1
Tobermory Way. DE24 19 G5
Tonbridge Dri. DE24 21 F3
Top Manor Clo. DE72 17 G3
Topley Gdns. DE21 10 D4
Torridon Clo. DE24 19 H4
Tower St. DE24 20 D2
Towle Clo. DE72 17 F6
Traffic St. DE1 6 D5
Trafford Way. DE23 19 F1
Tredegar Dri. DE21 11 E3
Trefoil Ct. DE23 18 D1
Tregaron Clo. DE21 11 F3
Tregony Way. DE24 19 G5
Trent Clo. DE24 19 G6
Trent Dri. DE23 19 G3
Trent Rise. DE21 16 D3
Trent St. DE24 21 F1
*Trentbridge Ct,
 Taverners Cres. DE23 19 F1
Trenton Dri. DE21 16 A2
Trenton Grn. DE21 15 H1
Tresillian Clo. DE22 9 E3
Treveris CloL. DE21 16 D3
Trevone Ct. DE24 21 H3
Trinity St. DE1 6 D5
Troon Clo. DE3 12 A4
Trowbridge Clo. DE21 10 C4
Trowels La. DE22 13 F3
Truro Cres. DE21 10 C5
Trusley Gdns. DE23 19 F3
Tudor Rd. DE21 15 G1
Tufnell Gdns. DE24 13 E1
Tulla Clo. DE24 19 G6
Turner St. DE24 20 D3
Tuxford Clo. DE21 11 E4
Tweedsmuir Clo. DE21 10 D4
Twickenham Dri. DE22 13 E2
Twin Oaks Clo. DE23 18 C2
Twyford St. DE23 6 C6
Tynedale Chase. DE24 19 F6

Uffa Magna. DE3 12 B6
Ullswater Clo. DE21 10 B4
Ullswater Dri. DE21 16 C2
Underhill Av. DE23 20 A2
Underhill Clo. DE23 19 H2
Upchurch Clo. DE3 12 A4
Uplands Av. DE23 19 F2
Uplands Gdns. DE23 13 H5
Upper Bainbrigge St.
 DE23 14 B5
Upper Boundary Rd.
 DE22 13 G3
Upper Dale Rd. DE23 14 B6
Upper Hollow. DE23 13 F6
Upper Moor Rd. DE24 20 D3
Urie Pl. DE24 21 E2
Uttoxeter New Rd. DE22 13 E4
Uttoxeter Old Rd. DE1 13 G3
Uttoxeter Rd. DE3 12 B6

Vale Mills. DE22 6 A6
Vale St. DE23 14 B5
Valley Rd. DE21 15 H2
Valley Rd. DE23 13 G6
Vancouver Av. DE21 16 C4
Varley St. DE24 20 D2
Vauxhall Av. DE24 13 E1
Verbena Dri. DE23 19 F4
Vermont Dri. DE21 16 B2
Vernon Dri. DE21 16 D4
Vernon St. DE1 13 H2
Vestry Rd. DE21 10 C3
Vetchfield Clo. DE24 19 H6

Vicarage Av. DE23 14 A5
Vicarage Ct. DE3 12 B6
Vicarage Dri. DE21 15 G1
Vicarage Rd. DE3 12 A5
Vicarage Rd. DE3 21 F6
Vicarwood Av. DE22 9 F4
Victor Av. DE22 9 E6
Victoria Av. DE72 17 F5
Victoria Clo. DE3 12 C4
Victoria St. DE1 6 C4
Victory Rd. DE24 20 B2
Village St. DE23 19 HI
Vincent Av. DE21 16 D4
Vincent St. DE23 14 A6
Vine Clo. DE23 19 E1
Viola Clo. DE21 11 F3
Violet St. DE23 14 B6
Vivian St. DE1 9 G6
Vulcan St. DE23 14 C6

Wade Av. DE23 13 F5
Wade Dri. DE3 13 F5
Wade St. DE23 13 F5
Wadebridge Gro. DE24 21 H3
Wakami Cres. DE73 21 F5
Walbrook Rd. DE23 14 B6
Waldene Dri. DE24 21 G3
Waldorf Av. DE24 21 F1
Waldorf Clo. DE24 21 G2
Walker La. DE1 6 B2
Wallace St. DE22 13 F2
Wallfields Clo. DE6 18 B5
Walnut Av. DE24 21 G2
Walnut St. DE24 20 C2
Walpole St. DE21 15 E1
Walsham Ct. DE21 10 B5
Walter St. DE1 13 H1
Waltham Av. DE24 20 A4
Walthamstow Dri. DE22 13 E2
Walton Av. DE24 20 D4
Walton Dri. DE23 19 G2
Walton Rd. DE21 15 F2
Wansfell Clo. DE3 12 C6
Ward St. DE22 13 H3
Wardlow Av. DE21 10 D5
Wardwick. DE1 6 B3
Warner St. DE23 6 A6
Warner St. DE22 12 B6
Warren St. DE24 21 F1
Warwick Av. DE23 13 G5
Warwick St. DE24 15 E5
Washington Av. DE21 16 A1
Waterford Dri. DE21 15 G3
Watergo La. DE3 18 B2
Waterloo Ct. DE1 6 D1
Watermeadow Rd. DE22 21 F4
Waterside Clo. DE22 9 G4
Watson Gdns. DE1 6 A1
Watson St. DE1 13 G1
Watten Clo. DE3 19 H6
Waveney Clo. DE24 9 G1
Waverley St. DE24 20 C2
Wayfaring Rd. DE21 10 D4
Wayzgoose Dri. DE21 14 D2
Weavers Clo. DE72 17 G6
Weavers Grn. DE3 12 A6
Webster St. DE1 6 B5
Weirfield Rd. DE22 9 F4
Welbeck Dri. DE22 8 D3
Well St. DE1 6 B1
Welland Clo. DE3 12 B4
Wellesley Av. DE23 19 G2
*Wellington Cres,
 Wellington St. DE1 14 D4
Wellington St. DE1 14 D4
Wells Clo. DE23 18 C1
Wells Rd. DE3 12 C5
Welney Clo. DE3 12 B6
Welshpool Rd. DE21 10 B4
Welwyn Av. DE24 21 E4
Welwyn Av. DE22 8 D3
Wembley Gdns. DE22 12 D2
Wendover Clo. DE3 12 A6
Wenlock Clo. DE3 12 C6
Wensley Dri. DE21 16 D4
Wensleydale Wk. DE24 21 H2
Wentworth Clo. DE3 12 C6
Werburgh Clo. DE21 16 C3
Werburgh St. DE22 6 A5
Wesley Rd. DE24 21 G3
Wesley St. DE72 17 F2
Wessington Mews. DE22 9 E5
West Av. DE21 6 A1
West Av. DE73 21 E5
West Bank Av. DE22 9 E5
West Bank Clo. DE22 9 E5
West Dri. DE3 12 A5
West Dri. DE21 16 D4
West Gro. DE23 20 D3

West Lawn. DE65 18 B6
West Park Rd. DE22 9 E5
West Rd. DE21 16 B2
West Row. DE22 9 F4
West Service Rd. DE21 15 G5
West View Av. DE23 19 E1
Westbank Rd. DE22 9 E1
Westbourne Park. DE22 12 C1
Westbury Ct. DE22 13 G4
Westbury St. DE22 13 G4
Westcroft Av. DE23 19 G4
Westdene Av. DE24 20 D3
Western Rd. DE23 14 B4
Western Rd. DE3 12 B5
Westgreen Av. DE24 20 D4
Westhall Rd. DE3 12 B4
Westleigh Av. DE22 13 F2
Westminster St. DE24 21 F1
Westmorland Clo. DE1 14 D2
Weston Park Av. DE24 20 D5
Weston Park Rd. DE24 20 D5
Westwood Dri. DE24 20 D3
Wetherby Rd. DE24 20 D1
Wey Acres. DE72 17 F6
Wharfedale Clo. DE22 9 G2
Wheatcroft Way. DE23 9 H4
Wheatland Clo. DE24 19 F1
*Wheatsheaf Clo,
 Ryegrass Rd. DE21 11 F3
Wheeldon Av. DE22 9 E6
Whenby Clo. DE3 12 A5
Whernside Clo. DE24 21 H2
Whinbush Av. DE24 21 E4
Whiston St. DE23 14 B5
Whitaker Gdns. DE23 13 G5
Whitaker Rd. DE23 13 G5
Whitaker St. DE23 14 C5
Whitby Av. DE21 10 A4
White St. DE22 9 E6
White Way. DE22 9 E4
Whitecross Gdns. DE1 13 H1
Whitecross St. DE1 13 H1
Whitehouse Clo. DE24 20 D5
Whitehurst St. DE24 20 D2
Whitmore Rd. DE21 15 F1
Whitstable Clo. DE23 19 G2
Whittington St. DE23 20 D3
Whittlebury Dri. DE23 18 D2
Whitwell Gdns. DE21 21 H3
Whyteleafe Gro. DE21 11 E4
Wickersley Clo. DE22 9 E3
Widdybank Clo. DE22 8 C4
Wigmore Clo. DE3 12 A5
Wild St. DE1 13 G2
Wildsmith St. DE24 21 F1
Wilfred St. DE23 14 C5
Wilkins Dri. DE24 20 D2
Willesden Av. DE22 12 D1
Willetts Rd. DE21 11 E6
William St. DE1 6 A1
Willn St. DE23 14 B6
Willow Clo. DE72 9 F4
Willow Croft. DE24 21 H4
Willow Row. DE1 6 A2
Willowcroft Rd. DE21 16 C4
Willowherb Clo. DE21 19 H6
Willows End Clo. DE65 18 B6
Willson Av. DE23 19 F1
Willson Rd. DE23 . 19 F1
Wilmington Av. DE24 21 G4
Wilmore Rd. DE24 20 A3
Wilmot Av. DE21 15 F2
Wilmot St. DE1 6 C5
Wilmslow Dri. DE21 11 E5
Wilson Clo. DE3 18 A1
Wilson St. DE1 10 C5
Wilson St. DE1 6 B4
Wilsthorpe Rd. DE21 15 G1
Wilton Clo. DE24 19 F6
Wiltshire Rd. DE21 10 B6
Wimbledon Clo. DE22 12 D1
Wimbourne Clo. DE73 21 F6
Wimpole Gdns. DE21 13 E1
Wincanton Clo. DE24 19 H4
Winchcombe Way. DE21 11 E3
Winchester Cres. DE21 10 B5
Windermere Cres. DE22 9 E3
Windermere Dri. DE21 16 C2
Windley Cres. DE22 9 F4
Windmill Clo. DE72 17 G2
Windmill Hill La. DE22 13 F2
Windmill La. DE24 21 H4
Windsor Av. DE23 19 E1
Windsor Ct. DE72 17 G6
Windsor Ct. DE22 12 B4
Windsor Dri. DE21 16 D2
Wingerworth Pk Rd.
 DE21 16 C3

Wingfield Dri. DE21 1
Winslow Grn. DE21 1
Winster Rd. DE21 1
Wintergreen Dri. DE23 1
Wisgreaves Rd. DE24 2
Witham Dri. DE23 1
Witney Clo. DE24 2
Woburn Pl. DE22 .1
Wolfa St. DE22
Wollaton Rd. DE21 1
Wolverley Grange.
 DE24 2
Wood Rd,
 Chaddesden. DE21 1
Wood Rd,
 Spondon. DE21 1
Woodale Clo. DE1
Woodale Clo. DE23 1
Woodbeck Ct. DE21 1
*Woodchester Dri,
 Keldolme La. DE24 2
Woodcote Way. DE23 1
Woodcroft. DE23 1
Woodford Rd. DE24
Woodhall Dri. DE23
Woodhurst Clo. DE21 1
Woodland Av. DE72 1
Woodland Rd. DE23
Woodlands Av. DE24 2
Woodlands Rd. DE22
Woodminton Dri. DE73 2
Woodrising Clo. DE21 1
Woodroffe Walk. DE23 1
Woods La. DE22
Woodside Dri. DE24
Woodsorrel Dri. DE21
Woodstock Clo. DE22
Woodthorne Av. DE24 2
Woodthorpe Av. DE21 1
*Woodwards Clo,
 Ballards Way. DE72 1
Woolrych St. DE23
Worcester Cres. DE21 1
Wordsworth Av. DE24
Wordsworth Dri. DE24 2
Wragley Way. DE24
Wren Park Clo. DE65 1
Wretham Clo. DE3
Wroxham Clo. DE24
Wyaston Clo. DE22
Wye St. DE24 2
Wyndham St. DE24
Wynton Av. DE24
Wyvern Way. DE21

Yarrow Clo. DE24
Yarwell Clo. DE21
Yates Dri. DE23
Yates St. DE23
Yeovil Clo. DE24 2
Yew Tree Av. DE72
Yew Tree Av. DE23
Yewdale Gro. DE21
York Rd. DE21
York St. DE1
Youlgreave Clo. DE21
Young St. DE23
Ypres Rd. DE22

Zetland Cres. DE24

CASTLE DONNINGTON

Ambassador Rd. DE74 2
Apiary Gate. DE74 2
Argosy Rd. DE74 2
Ashby Rd. DE74 2
Aston Av. DE74 2
Back La. DE74 2
Bakewell. DE74 2
Barroon. DE74 2
Bentley Rd. DE74 2
Beverley Rd. DE74 2
Bondgate. DE74 2
Borough St. DE74 2
Bosworth Rd. DE74 2
Campion Hill. DE74 2
Carrs Clo. DE74 2
Castle Hill. DE74 2
Cavendish Clo. DE74 2
Cedar Rd. DE74 2
Charnock Hill. DE74 2
Charnwood Av. DE74 2
Cheriborough Rd. DE74 2
Church La, Castle
 Donington. DE74 2

ch La,
ckington. DE74 25 E1
ch St. DE74 25 G1
gun St. DE74 24 C2
well Clo. DE74 24 B2
tree Clo. DE74 24 B3
way. DE74 24 B1
acre Av. DE74 25 F1
en La. DE74 24 C2
worth Rd. DE74 24 B4
e Cote. DE74 24 C2
way. DE74 24 C2
n Rd. DE74 24 C3
ers Clo. DE74 24 B2
rook Dri. DE74 24 A2
Rd. DE74 24 A1
len Cres. DE74 24 C2
ge Dri. DE74 24 B2
es Gate. DE74 24 D6
Farm Clo. DE74 24 C2
am Fields. DE74 24 C3
ourt Pl. DE74 24 C2
ey Ct. DE74 24 C2
ey Rd. DE74 24 C3
ings St. DE74 24 C3
ton Dri. DE74 24 C2
thorn Rd. DE74 24 C1
Irigg Clo. DE74 24 B1
mington Ct,
Main St. DE74 25 E1
ington Hill. DE74 24 D2
ington La. DE74 25 F1
St. DE74 24 B4
Top. DE74 24 C4
ide. DE74 24 C2
ingdon Dri. DE74 24 B2
ns La. DE74 25 F6
and Clo. DE74 24 C2
e Hill. DE74 24 C2
ington Rd. DE74 25 E1
ian Pl. DE74 24 B2
loun Pl. DE74 24 B2
St,
mington. DE74 25 E1
St,
ckington. DE74 25 F2
ket Pl. DE1 24 C2
ket St. DE74 24 C2
dow Cres. DE74 24 A2
on Rd. DE74 24 A2
a Dale. DE74 24 D2
tford Mews. DE74 24 D2
tieth Pl. DE74 24 C2
nt Pleasant. DE74 24 C3
ard Av. DE74 24 C3
Av. DE74 24 A2
lock Clo. DE74 24 A2
Av. DE74 24 B2
La. DE74 24 A2
tree La. DE74 24 B2
ensway. DE74 24 B2
don Clo. DE74 24 B1
y Lea. DE74 24 A2
h Av. DE74 24 C3
nnes La. DE74 24 C3
dwards Rd. DE74 24 C3
a Clo. DE74 24 B2
iol La. DE74 24 B2
ld Cres. DE74 24 B3
Clo. DE74 24 B1
t La. DE74 24 A1
al Hill. DE74 24 A1
xie Av. DE74 24 B4
on Rd. DE74 24 C1
nton Clo. DE74 24 B2
e Hill. DE74 24 C3
brook Clo. DE74 24 A2
n River. DE74 24 C5
more Rd. DE74 24 C1
ard Clo. DE74 24 B2
Biggin. DE74 24 C2
Green. DE74 24 D6
Hollow. DE74 24 C2
Horse Shoes,
Main St. DE74 25 E1
Moat. DE74 24 C2
Spinney. DE74 24 B2
Spital. DE74 24 B1
all Rd. DE74 24 C2
es Pastures. DE74 24 B3
ria St. DE74 24 C1
ount Rd. DE74 24 D6
on Hill. DE74 24 C1
am Rd. DE74 24 C1
mill Clo. DE74 24 C3

CHELLASTON

Aston Clo. DE73 27 C2
Aston La. DE73 27 C1
Back La. DE73 27 C1
Barley Croft. DE73 27 C1
Bensley Clo. DE73 27 B1
Boyd Gro. DE73 27 C2
*Bradmoor Gro,
Netherside. DE73 27 C1
Bridle Clo. DE73 27 C2
Chapel La. DE73 27 C2
Chellaston Pk Ct. DE73 27 B1
Church Clo. DE73 27 C1
Crowland Dri. DE73 27 C1
Davids Clo. DE73 27 B2
Derby Rd. DE73 27 B1
Derby Southern Bypass.
DE73 27 A3
Fellowlands Way. DE73 27 C1
Filbert Walk. DE73 27 C2
Foxdell Way. DE73 27 C1
Glenwood Rd. DE73 27 C2
Green Av. DE73 27 C1
Groves Nook. DE73 27 B1
Hawksdale Clo. DE73 27 C1
High St. DE73 27 C1
Hillnook Clo. DE73 27 C2
Hollymoor Dri. DE73 27 B1
Lady Mantle Clo. DE73 27 B1
Lee Farm Clo. DE73 27 B1
Lincoln Grn. DE73 27 B1
Lockington Clo. DE73 27 B1
Manor Rd. DE73 27 B1
Maple Dri. DE73 27 B1
Meadow Way. DE73 27 C2
Middlebeck Clo. DE73 27 B1
Mill Moor Clo. DE73 27 B1
Moyne Gdns. DE73 27 C2
Netherside Dri. DE73 27 C1
Newgate Clo. DE73 27 D1
*Nothills Clo,
Hawksdale Clo. DE73 27 C1
Orchard Way. DE73 27 C1
Parklands Dri. DE73 27 B1
Parkway. DE73 27 C2
Penhaligans Clo. DE73 27 B1
Penhaligans Wk. DE73 27 B1
Pit Close La. DE73 27 C1
Priory Clo. DE73 27 C2
Ridgeway. DE73 27 C2
Rye Butts. DE73 27 B1
St Peters Rd. DE73 27 C1
Sandyhill Clo. DE73 27 C1
School La. DE73 27 C1
Second Av. DE73 27 C2
Sinfin Moor La. DE73 27 A1
Sladelands Dri. DE73 27 C1
Smallmeer Clo. DE73 27 C1
Snelsmoor La. DE73 27 B1
Stadmoor Clo. DE73 27 B1
Station Clo. DE73 27 B2
Station Rd. DE73 27 B2
Swarkestone Rd. DE73 27 B3
Tarina Clo. DE73 27 C1
Thurstone Furlong.
DE73 27 B1
Townsend Gro. DE73 27 C1
Tudorfield Clo. DE73 27 C2
Walnut Clo. DE73 27 C1
Warrendale Ct. DE73 27 C2
Weston Rise. DE73 27 C1
Willowbrook Grange.
DE73 27 C1
Wimbourne Clo. DE73 27 C1
Woodbridge Clo. DE73 27 B1
Woodgate Dri. DE73 27 C2
Woodlands La. DE73 27 C2
Yews Clo. DE73 27 C1

DRAYCOTT

Albert Rd. DE72 27 C5
Arthur St. DE72 27 A5
Attewell Clo. DE72 27 C5
Belvoir Clo. DE72 27 D5
Breaston Ind Est. DE72 27 D5
Bridge Field. DE72 27 D5
Burlington Av. DE72 27 D4
Churchill Clo. DE72 27 D4
Cleveland Av. DE72 27 B5
Delamere Clo. DE72 27 D4
Derby Rd. DE72 27 A4
Derwent St. DE72 27 B6
Draycott Rd. DE72 27 D5
Earlswood Clo. DE72 27 D4
Elvaston St. DE72 27 C5
Far Croft. DE72 27 D3
Festival Av. DE72 27 D5
Fowler St. DE72 27 C5
Garfield Av. DE72 27 B5
Gertrude Rd. DE72 27 B5
Gregory Av. DE72 27 C5
Harrington St. DE72 27 C5
Hayes Av. DE72 27 C5
Hills Rd. DE72 27 C5
Hind Av. DE72 27 D5
Holly Clo. DE72 27 B6
Holmes Rd. DE72 27 D4
Hopwell Rd. DE72 27 B4
INDUSTRIAL ESTATES:
Breaston Ind Est.
DE72 27 D5
Lime Gro. DE72 27 A5
Lodge St. DE72 27 B6
McNeil Gro. DE72 27 B6
Mapleton Rd. DE72 27 B5
Market St. DE72 27 B5
Meadow Clo. DE72 27 B5
Mills Clo. DE72 27 B5
Milner Av. DE72 27 B6
Plackett Clo. DE72 27 D4
Queens Ct. DE72 27 B5
St Marys Av. DE72 27 B5
Sawley Rd. DE72 27 C5
South St. DE72 27 B6
Spring Clo. DE72 27 D5
Station Rd. DE72 27 C5
Stevenson Av. DE72 27 B5
Sydney Rd. DE72 27 B5
The Crescent. DE72 27 D5
The Croft. DE72 27 B6
The Green. DE72 27 B5
Thoresby Cres. DE72 27 C5
Town End Rd. DE72 27 C5
Victoria Av. DE72 27 B5
Victoria Rd. DE72 27 B5
Villa St. DE72 27 C5
Walk Clo. DE72 27 B6
Wallis Clo. DE72 27 B5
Walter St. DE72 27 A5
West Av. DE72 27 A5
Wilne Rd. DE72 27 B6

DUFFIELD

Avenue Rd. DE56 26 B2
Breedon Av. DE56 26 B4
Broadway. DE56 26 B4
Broom Clo. DE56 26 B4
*Canterbury Clo, New
Zealand La. DE56 26 B4
Castle Hill. DE56 26 C2
Castle Orchard. DE56 26 C2
Cavendish Clo. DE56 26 B4
Chadfield Rd. DE56 26 C1
Champion Hill. DE56 26 C3
Chapel St. DE56 26 C3
Chestnut Clo. DE56 26 C5
Chevin Bank. DE56 26 B1
Chevin Rd. DE56 26 B2
Chevin Vale. DE56 26 C1
Church Walk. DE56 26 D5
Crown St. DE56 26 C3
Cumberhills Rd. DE56 26 A5
Curzon Clo. DE56 26 C3
Curzon La. DE56 26 B4
*Deferrers Ct,
Tamworth St. DE56 26 C3
Derby Rd. DE56 26 C1
Devonshire Dri. DE56 26 B4
Donald Hawley Way.
DE56 26 D4
Duck Island. DE56 26 C3
Eaton Ct. DE56 26 C5
Ecclesbourne Av. DE56 26 C4
Ecclesbourne Clo. DE56 26 C4
Eyes Ct. DE56 26 C4
Fairlawns. DE56 26 A4
Ferrers Cres. DE56 26 A4
Fisher La. DE56 26 C3
Gilbert Cres. DE56 26 C5
Golf La. DE56 26 C1
Granville Clo. DE56 26 C4
Hall Farm Rd. DE56 26 C4
Hazel Gro. DE56 26 B4
Hazeldene Clo. DE56 26 B1
Hazelwood Rd. DE56 26 A1
Hill Vw. DE56 26 B3
Holloway Rd. DE56 26 B3
King St. DE56 26 C2
Lime Av. DE56 26 C2
Lodge Clo. DE56 26 C4
Makeney Rd. DE56 26 D5
Marsden Clo. DE56 26 B4
Mayfair Clo. DE56 26 C2
Meadow Vale. DE56 26 A3
Meadows Croft. DE56 26 B4
Melbourne Clo. DE56 26 C4
Milford Rd. DE56 26 C3
Nether Clo. DE56 26 B4
New Zealand La. DE56 26 B4
Oak Clo. DE56 26 C4
Old Hall Av. DE56 26 B4
Old Mill Clo. DE56 26 B3
Park Rd. DE56 26 B4
Philips Croft. DE56 26 C2
Richmond Av. DE56 26 B1
St Alkmunds Clo. DE56 26 C2
St Alkmunds Way. DE56 26 C2
St Ronans Av. DE56 26 C4
Scarsdale Rd. DE56 26 B4
Snake La. DE56 26 B3
Springfield Dri. DE56 26 B4
Station App. DE56 26 C3
Station Rd. DE56 26 C4
Stiles Walk. DE56 26 D3
*Tamworth Rise,
Tamworth St. DE56 26 C3
Tamworth St. DE56 26 C3
Tamworth Ter. DE56 26 C3
The Pastures. DE56 26 C4
Town St. DE56 26 C3
Vicarage La. DE56 26 C2
Village Ct. DE56 26 C3
Wiltra Gro. DE56 26 D4
Wirksworth Rd. DE56 26 A3

HEANOR LOSCOE

Abbott St. DE75 23 E4
Adale Rd. DE75 22 C5
Adams Clo. DE75 22 D6
Admiral Clo. DE75 23 E4
Aldercar By-Pass. NG16 23 F1
Aldercar La. NG16 23 H1
Aldreds La. DE75 23 G4
Allandale Rd. DE75 23 E3
Amber Ct. DE75 23 E4
Amber Dri. NG16 23 H3
Andrews Dri. NG16 23 G2
Ardsley Clo. DE75 23 G3
Argyle St. NG16 23 H2
Ashforth Av. DE75 23 G5
Ashmount Rd. NG16 23 H3
Astcote Clo. DE75 23 G4
Avis Av. DE75 23 F6
Bailey Brook Cres.
NG16 23 G2
Bailey Brook Dri. NG16 23 G2
Bailey Brook Ind Est.
NG16 23 H3
Bailey Brook Wk. NG16 23 G2
Baker Av. DE75 23 F6
Banks Burn Clo. DE75 22 D4
Bassford Av. DE75 23 F3
Belfield Ct. DE75 22 C1
Berle Av. DE75 23 E3
Bestwick Av. DE75 23 H4
Birchfield Park. DE75 23 F6
Birchwood. DE75 22 D2
Bircum Shaw Rd. DE75 23 E4
Brampton Av. DE75 23 G3
Breach Rd, Denby
Common. DE75 22 A2
Breach Rd,
Heanor. DE75 23 G5
Broadway. DE75 23 E4
Brockhall Rise. DE75 23 G4
Brook St. DE75 23 C1
Brooklands Av. DE75 23 F3
Burns St. DE75 23 F3
Burnt House Rd. DE75 22 D4
Burton St. DE75 23 E3
Buxton Av. DE75 23 F6
Buxton Grn. DE75 23 F6
Calladine Clo. DE75 22 D3
Carlton Clo. DE75 23 G3
Carlyle Pl. DE75 23 E3
Carlyle St. DE75 23 E3
Castle Vw. NG16 23 G1
Chapel St. DE75 23 G5
Chestnut Bank. NG16 23 G2
Chestnut Rd. DE75 23 G2
Church St. DE75 23 G2
Church Vw. DE75 22 C2
Claramount Rd. DE75 23 G4
Clarke Av. DE75 22 D3
Claxton St. DE75 3 E4
Claxton Ter. DE75 23 E4
Clay La. DE75 23 F3
Clayton Gro. DE75 22 D1
Codnor-Denby La. DE75 22 A1
Coppice Dri. DE75 23 F6
Corfield Av. DE75 23 G3
Cottage Gdns. DE75 22 D3
Cromford Clo. NG16 23 H1
Cromford Rd. NG16 23 G1
Daltons Clo. NG16 23 G1
*Darfield Dri,
Brampton Av. DE75 23 G3
Deepdale Ct. DE75 23 E5
Delves Rd. DE75 22 D5
Denby Common. DE75 22 A3
Derby Rd. DE75 22 D4
Dodford Ct. DE75 23 G4
Douglas Av. DE75 22 D3
Draycott Clo. DE75 22 C1
Dumbles La. DE75 22 A3
East Nelson St. DE75 23 E3
Eastview Ter. NG16 23 H2
Ebenezer St. NG16 23 H2
Edward St. NG16 23 H2
Egreaves Av. DE75 22 C1
Ella Bank Rd. DE75 23 G4
Elmsfield Av. DE75 23 G3
England Cres. DE75 23 G3
Fairview. DE75 23 E4
Fall Rd. DE75 23 E3
Fast St. DE75 23 G5
Flamstead Av. DE75 22 C2
Fletcher St. DE75 23 E3
Ford Av. DE75 22 C1
Frederic Av. DE75 23 F6
Frost Av. NG16 23 G2
Furnace La. DE75 22 D1
Garnett Av. DE75 23 F3
George St. NG16 23 H2
Gillot St. DE75 23 G5
Gladstone Av. DE75 23 F3
Gladstone St. DE75 23 F3
Glue La. DE75 22 C3
Godfrey St. DE75 23 E4
Godkin Dri. NG16 23 G1
Grace Cres. DE75 23 F4
Grammer St. DE75 22 B1
Grandfield St. DE75 22 D1
Greenacre Av. DE75 23 G3
Greenfields. NG16 23 G1
Greggs Av. DE75 23 F3
Gregory Dri. NG16 23 G2
Groome Av. DE75 22 C2
Hallington Dri. DE75 22 D4
Hampden St. NG16 23 H2
Hands Rd. DE75 23 F4
Hardy Barn. DE75 23 G6
Harold Av. NG16 23 H2
Hassock Lane N. DE75 23 H6
Hazel Clo. DE75 23 G3
Heanor Gate Rd. DE75 22 D5
Heanor Rd, Denby
Common. DE75 22 A2
Heanor Rd,
Heanor Gate. DE75 22 B6
Heanor Rd,
Loscoe. DE75 22 D2
Heyford Ct. DE75 23 G5
High St, Heanor. DE75 23 E3
High St, Loscoe. DE75 23 C1
Hill Rd. DE75 23 E4
Hillside. NG16 23 G3
Hogbarn La. DE75 23 E1
Holbrook St. DE75 23 G3
Holmes Clo. NG16 23 G2
Holmes St. DE75 23 G2
Holmesfield Dri. DE75 23 F5
Homestead. NG16 23 H1
Horsley Cres. NG16 23 G2
Howitt St. DE75 23 F4
Huftons Ct. DE75 23 G6
Huftons Dri. DE75 23 G6
Hunt Av. DE75 23 F3
Ilkeston Rd. DE75 23 F4
INDUSTRIAL ESTATES:
Bailey Brook Ind Est.
NG16 23 H3
Sawmills Ind Pk. DE75 23 E2
Joan Av. DE75 23 E3
John St. DE75 23 E3
Johns Pl. DE75 23 E4
Johnson Dri. DE75 23 H4
Julie Av. DE75 23 H4
Kew Cres. DE75 23 H5
Kings Clo. DE75 23 F6
Kingsway. DE75 22 D4
Kirkham Clo. DE75 23 E5

Kirkman Rd. DE75	22 C1	Newham Ct. DE75	23 G4	Sawmills Ind Pk. DE75	23 E2

Kirkman Rd. DE75 22 C1
Lacy Fields Rd. DE75 23 G4
Lake Av. DE75 22 D1
Lawn Clo. DE75 23 F3
Leafy La. DE75 23 G4
Lee La. DE75 23 H4
Leniscar Av. DE75 22 C2
Lockton Av. DE75 23 E5
Loscoe Grange. DE75 22 D2
Loscoe Rd. DE75 23 E3
Loscoe-Denby La. DE75 22 B2
Lower Claramount Rd.
DE75 23 G4
Lower Dunstead Rd.
NG16 23 H3
Lower Gladstone St.
DE75 23 E2
Lowlands Lea. DE75 23 F3
Mansfield Rd. DE75 23 F4
Maple Gdns. DE75 22 D4
Marina Rd. DE75 22 C5
Market Pl. DE75 23 F4
Market St. DE75 23 E4
Marshall St. DE75 23 G3
Mayfield Av. DE75 23 E4
Midland Rd. DE75 23 E3
Mill Rd. DE75 23 G5
Millbank. DE7. DE75 23 G5
Milward Rd. DE75 22 D3
Mitchell Av. NG16 23 G2
Mount St. DE75 23 E4
Mundy St. DE75 23 E4
Mundys Dri. DE75 23 F5
Nelson St. DE75 23 E3

Newham Ct. DE75 23 G4
Newlands Dri. DE75 23 F3
Nook End Rd. DE75 23 E4
North St. NG16 23 H2
Northern Rd. DE75 22 D3
Oak Av. NG16 23 H1
Oaklands Av. DE75 23 G3
Old Coppice Side. DE75 23 E6
Oliver Clo. DE75 23 H3
Orchard Rise. DE75 23 F3
Orchard St. NG16 23 H3
Ormonde St. NG16 23 H1
Ormonde Ter. NG16 23 H1
Owers Av. DE75 23 F6
Park St. DE75 22 D3
Park Vw. DE75 22 D4
Peach St. DE75 23 E5
Peatburn Av. DE75 22 D4
Peel St. NG16 23 H3
Piatts Av. DE75 22 D4
Pine Av. DE75 23 G2
Plumptre Rd. NG16 23 H1
Poynter Clo. DE75 22 D4
Prospect Rd. DE75 23 G5
Purchase Av. DE75 22 D3
Queens Av. DE75 22 D3
Ray Av. DE75 23 E4
Ray St. DE75 23 E4
Red Lion Sq. DE75 23 E4
Regent St. NG16 23 H2
Ridgeway. DE75 23 G6
Roper Av. DE75 23 F5
Rosewood Cres. DE75 23 H3
St Laurence Clo. DE75 23 F4

Sawmills Ind Pk. DE75 23 E2
Saxton Av. DE75 23 F3
Sedgewick St. NG16 23 H3
Sheldon Rd. DE75 22 C1
Sinclair Clo. DE75 22 D5
Slack La. DE75 23 E5
Smeeton St. DE75 23 H4
Smith Dri. NG16 23 G2
Sovereign Way. DE75 22 D4
Spring La. DE75 23 E4
Stainsby Av. DE75 23 E5
Stamford St. DE57 23 E3
Starthe Bank. DE75 23 G4
Station Rd. NG16 23 H3
Stoddard Dri. DE75 23 F4
Sunningdale Av. DE75 23 F6
Tantum Av. DE75 22 D1
Taylor La. DE75 22 D2
The Beeches. DE75 22 C5
The Hamlet. DE75 23 E3
The Meadows. DE75 23 E4
The Nook. DE75 22 C1
Thistle Green Clo. DE75 23 H4
Thompson St. NG16 23 H2
Thorpe Rd. DE75 23 E4
Thorpehill Dri. DE75 23 F6
Tudor Falls. DE75 23 E3
Turner Av. NG16 23 G2
Turton Clo. NG16 23 G2
Twyford Clo. DE75 22 D5
Upper Barn Clo. DE75 23 F3
Upper Dunstead Rd.
NG16 23 H2
Upper Nelson St. DE75 23 E4

Upton Clo. DE75 23 G4
Victoria Av. DE75 22 D4
Watkinson St. DE75 22 D3
Watson Av. DE75 23 F3
Welldon St. DE75 22 B1
Wellington St. DE75 22 D3
Wentworth Croft. DE75 23 G3
West St, Heanor. DE75 22 D3
West St,
Langley Mill. NG16 23 H3
Western Dri. DE75 23 F5
Westfield Av. DE75 23 F5
Weston St. DE75 23 G5
Whysall St. DE75 23 E4
Wilmot St. DE75 23 E5
Wilson Av. DE75 22 C1
Windsor Clo. DE75 23 E3
Woodend Rd. DE75 23 E3

LITTLE EATON

Alfreton Rd. DE21 7 C6
Barley Clo. DE21 7 B5
Bermuda Av. DE21 7 C6
Brooks Hollow. DE21 7 B5
Buxton Dri. DE21 7 C3
Campwood Clo. DE21 7 B6
Chatsworth Dri. DE21 7 C3
Church La. DE21 7 B5
Coxbench Rd. DE21 7 D1
Crabtree Hill. DE21 7 B5
Croft End. DE21 7 C5

Derby Rd. DE21
Duffield Bank. DE21
Duffield Rd. DE21
Eaton Bank. DE21
Haddon Dri. DE21
Highfields Rd. DE21
Holm Av. DE21
Horsley La. DE21
Little Eaton By-Pass.
DE21
Moor La. DE21
Morley La. DE21
New Inn La. DE21
New St. DE21
Old Barn Clo. DE21
Park Clo. DE21
Park View. DE21
Port Way. DE21
Rigga La. DE21
Station Rd. DE21
The Chase. DE21
The Hawthorns. DE21
The Leys. DE21
The Oaks. DE21
The Town. DE21
Vicarage La. DE21
Westley Cres. DE21
Whittaker La. DE21
Woodlands Clo. DE21
Woodlea Gro. DE21